1,001 Ways to
Save Money . . .
and Still Have a
Dazzling Wedding

Sharon Naylor

Updated 3rd F

McGraw
Hill

New York   Chicago   San Francisco   Lisbon   London   Madrid   Mexico City
Milan   New Delhi   San Juan   Seoul   Singapore   Sydney   Toronto

The McGraw·Hill Companies

Library of Congress Cataloging-in-Publication Data

Naylor, Sharon.
    1,001 ways to save money . . . and still have a dazzling wedding / Sharon Naylor. —
3rd ed.
        p.   cm.
    Includes index.
    ISBN-13 978-0-07-161145-9 (alk. paper)
    ISBN-10 0-07-161145-2 (alk. paper)
    1. Weddings.   I. Title.   II. Title: One thousand one ways to save money . . .
and still have a dazzling wedding.   III. Title: One thousand and one ways to save
money . . . and still have a dazzling wedding.

BJ2051.N39   2009
395.2′2—dc22   2008034458

1 2 3 4 5 6 7 8 9 10 11 12 13 14 15 16 17 18 19 20 21   FGR/FGR   0 9 8

ISBN 978-0-07-161145-9
MHID   0-07-161145-2

McGraw-Hill books are available at special quantity discounts to use as premiums and sales
promotions or for use in corporate training programs. To contact a representative, please
visit the Contact Us pages at www.mhprofessional.com.

This book is printed on acid-free paper.

Contents

~ ACKNOWLEDGMENTS   v

~ PREFACE   vii

1. Your Engagement Celebration 1

2. Your Wedding Planning Team 13

3. Wedding Websites, Organizers, and Communication. 17

4. Finding Savings at Bridal Shows 33

5. Your Gift List and Bridal Registries. 39

6. Your Bridal Party 47

7. Setting a Budget 53

8. Timing Your Wedding. 61

9. Your Guest List 73

10. Your Ceremony Location 83

11. Your Reception Location 93

12. Religious, Spiritual, and Cultural Elements
    of the Ceremony. 101

13. Your Gown 109

14. *Your Shoes and Accessories* 127

15. *Dressing the Bridal Party* 139

16. *Dressing the Mothers of the Bride and Groom*............. 153

17. *Dressing the Men*.. 159

18. *Your Rings*... 167

19. *Invitations and Save-the-Date Cards* 179

20. *Destination Weddings* 195

21. *Flowers and Decorations*................................. 201

22. *Transportation for All* 223

23. *Music for the Ceremony*.................................. 233

24. *The Photographer and Videographer*...................... 237

25. *Wedding Programs and Printed Items* 255

26. *The Guest Book, Ring Pillows, and Other Items*........... 261

27. *Decorating the Reception* 265

28. *Planning the Menu* 269

29. *Beverages* 285

30. *The Cake*... 291

31. *Reception Entertainment* 305

32. *Wedding Favors* 315

33. *Keepsakes*.. 323

34. *Wedding Night Accommodations* 327

35. *Your Trousseau*... 329

36. *Guest Lodging* 333

37. *The Rehearsal Dinner*.................................... 337

38. *Your Personal Beauty Care*.............................. 341

39. *Gifts for Others*.. 347

⁓ Author's Note   353

⁓ Index   355

Acknowledgments

With tremendous gratitude to my editors at McGraw-Hill: Betsy Lancefield for being the first to bring this book into fruition, Sarah Pelz for bringing the newest version of this book to life, and Marisa L'Heureux for her expert work on design and production. My deepest thanks and love to my agent Meredith Bernstein for her guidance and for being the "Carrie Bradshaw" at my own wedding!

My heart bursts with gratitude for the wonderful friends and brides who contributed their ideas and inspirations: Jill Althouse-Wood, Pamela Bishop, Jennifer Stinson, Julie Weingarden, Oksana Yurchuk, and the many brides who attended my book-signings and lectures.

Acknowledgments

To all of the wonderfully helpful wedding professionals who allowed me to interview them for this book, including Rich Penrose of Dean Michaels Studio, Bill Chriswell and Alan Weinstein of The Park Savoy, Kathy Kucinski of Sweet Peas Flower Shoppe, Alyssa Tierney of Tierney's Bridal Salon, Sylvia Weinstock, Ron Ben-Israel, and Michelle and Henry Roth: no wonder you are the best in the business.

To my family, thank you for all of your support and love.

And for the first time . . . to my husband, Joe. That was a dazzling wedding we put on! Thank you for asking me to be your bride.

Preface

Congratulations on your engagement! This is a very exciting time for you both, since you're at the start of building your new life together. But first, your wedding! If you're like most brides, you're equally thrilled and terrified. On the one hand, weddings are a time of great love and family togetherness, the day when you join your lives together as one. That's the thrilling part. The "terrified" part comes in when you think about how much your dream wedding will cost. You may have heard friends talk about their fifty-thousand-dollar budgets, and seen them crumble when the financial strain hits them and their parents. People start fighting, credit cards get maxed out, and some wedding dreams have to be left out because there's just not enough money to make them possible.

Money doesn't have to wreck your wedding dreams! By using the tips in this book, you can get twice the wedding for your budget, or spend far less than the national averages. Take a look at what TheWeddingReport.com, a national wedding survey, says about the average cost of weddings now and in the future:

AVERAGE TOTAL WEDDING SPENDING					
2008	2009	2010	2011	2012	2013
$28,704	$29,614	$30,553	$31,522	$32,521	$33,552

Keep in mind that these are national averages, and that weddings in your region of the country can cost twice if not three times these figures. But don't be alarmed. You have in your hands the guide to reducing your wedding budget without revealing the cuts to others. You'll understand the various charges in each separate wedding industry such as flowers, catering, photography, and entertainment. With the insider advice in this book, you'll find out which questions to ask, which discounts to ask for, and what you can get for *free*.

Even better, you can share many of these ideas with your friends and family so that they too can save money related to wedding expenses. That's a big gift to your parents and bridal party members, so be sure to make notes in the margins, flag any tips you want to share with others, and use this book as your money-saving sidekick all the way through your wedding-planning process.

Planning a wedding is supposed to be fun! And you can make it fun when you find yourself celebrating the most recent way you beat your original budget estimates, when you negotiated a freebie from a vendor, and when you discovered a hidden charge that you were smart enough to have removed from your bill. Ready to get started? Let's rescue your wedding budget and start to put your Dream Day plans into motion!

GOLDEN RULES OF WEDDING COST-CUTTING

1. As the bride and groom, you have tremendous bargaining power. Wedding experts compete for the business of every wedding couple in your area, so they want to make you happy by working hard to meet your wedding budget. When they do a great job, you'll recommend them to all of your friends and family. So they have great incentive to work within your budget constraints and still give you great products and services!

2. You need to be a smart consumer. That means reading contracts carefully, researching vendors well, and

comparison shopping like crazy. Invest lots of time in these important steps, and you'll spend your money wisely.

3. Don't make plans or book sites or experts on impulse or when you're exhausted or stressed. You'll wind up wasting money.

4. Ask your friends and family members for referrals to the experts they worked with. Not only will you find out what it was really like to work with them, you may find out that their budget package really was quite wonderful!

5. Build a priority list of the top five categories where you'd like to spend the bulk of your wedding money—such as reception menu, flowers, gown, entertainment, and photos—and you'll then be able to cut more from the budgets of your less-favored items like limousines and invitations without it hurting too much. You don't want to feel like you're "cheaping out" on every area of your wedding plans, so allow yourselves permission to splurge on a few special elements of your day by shifting funds from other areas of your budget.

Your Priority List

1. _____
2. _____
3. _____
4. _____
5. _____

1

Your Engagement Celebration

You can shout your good news from the rooftop for free, but it's much better to put your engagement announcement in print. Here's how to save on this portion of your wedding budget.

The Engagement Photo

~ There's no need for a professionally taken engagement photo. Skip the pricey sitting with a pro and just have a friend take a series of great couple photos using a digital camera. A session with a professional photographer might cost more than one hundred dollars, while the DIY approach is *free*.

The Newspaper Announcement

∼ Submit your announcement and picture to newspapers that do not charge for publication in their announcement column.

∼ If your town's newspaper charges by the word, practice writing your announcement in the fewest words possible. One bride saved fifteen dollars just by revising and condensing.

∼ If your town's newspaper only charges a flat fee for the announcement, get your money's worth, and an even better memento, by writing a long entry filled with detail.

∼ Check the newspaper's website for graphic size, such as 300 dpi, and for guidance on how you should be posed. Some newspapers require that you're standing next to each other, not sitting on your fiance's lap. If you break the rules, they might print your announcement without the photo . . . and still charge you!

∼ Edit your engagement announcement well. You don't want to allow typographical errors on your part to be printed in the paper, insulting your future in-laws, whose names you've misspelled, and causing you to have to pay for an edited version of your announcement in the paper the following week.

ℐtationery Announcements

∼ Don't order your engagement announcements from a bridal salon or bridal shop. Those establishments are targeted specifically toward the bridal consumer, and that usually means you'll be paying top dollar.

∼ If you're ordering printed announcements of your engagement, shop around at stationery stores for the best prices. Look for special sales that can save you 10 percent, 20 percent, or more. Or go to discount invitation websites like invitations4sale .com, where you'll find Birchcraft, Carlson, and other brand-name invitation lines for 40 percent off retail . . . and they donate a percentage of your purchase to the Leukemia and Lymphoma Society. It's a win-win!

∼ Order a simple style of announcement. The price of a basic and very classy black print on white paper selection will go up if you choose a different typeface, color of print, or any additional graphics. Sometimes the savings can add up to 50 percent when you keep it simple.

⤳ Know exactly how many engagement announcements you'll need so you don't order too many. One bride overspent by fifty dollars (make that wasted fifty dollars) by ordering her announcements long before she had reached a firm number of recipients. The extra announcements now sit in a box in her closet.

⤳ Simply buy some high-quality paper by the pound at a discount or stationery store, and print your own announcements using a classy font on your home computer. Several excellent designed-paper sources are Paper Direct (paper direct.com), Botanical Paper Works (botanicalpaperworks .com), and Paper Access (paperaccess.com). Also, check your local Staples (staples.com) or OfficeMax (officemax.com) stores for their new wedding paper and envelope lines, often found in elegant styles for four to five dollars per pack of twenty-five.

⤳ Either print the announcements yourself, which is the least expensive way, or take a master copy to a discount print shop and have them do it for you (which can *save* you money when you don't have to burn through thirty-dollar ink cartridges on your home computer!). A great source to check out for invitation-design software is mountaincow.com where you'll find twenty-dollar software programs and inexpensive wedding clip-art programs for extra zing to your designs. This program allows you to design not just invitations but programs and place cards as well. At twenty dollars or so, that's a steal and a *big* jump over what other brides are paying for engagement and wedding invitations!

COMPARE AND SAVE

Store-ordered announcements $120

Homemade announcements plus discount
   print shop $45

Homemade plus home-copied announcements $30

∽ Perhaps the best news: if you're announcing the engagement at a party or gathering, you don't have to send out printed announcements at all. No one will miss them.

For my announcements, I raided an after-Christmas 50-percent-off sale for holiday stationery. Then I printed up announcements using my home computer and the holiday stationery, and I mailed them out the day after Christmas. They turned out lovely and perfect for the season.

—FRANCES

$\mathcal{Y}$*our Engagement Party*

Pop the corks and let the celebration begin! The engagement party is the kickoff of all of the once-in-a-lifetime events to come, so make this event extra special without breaking the bank.

~ Compare among store-bought engagement party invitations. The regular-sized ones are less expensive than the oversized ones because less card stock is needed and smaller invitations require less postage. Just be sure, though, that the invitation you choose reflects the level of formality of the engagement party.

~ If you're ordering your engagement party invitations from a printer, choose colors and fonts that are on their standard list. Many invitation companies offer additional designs, graphics, colors, and fonts at additional charges. Those are not needed. Go simple and elegant for this invitation.

~ Make your own engagement party invitations on your home computer with a classy font and your own clip art or digital graphics for decoration. For further savings, search for quality paper for these homemade invitations (see page 4 for a list of sources). Your comparison shopping may find the best values at a buy-by-the-pound paper source, and you can often get bargain-priced matching envelopes there, too!

~ EVite is fine for engagement party invitations—and it's free! Check your favorite free e-postcard site like hallmark.com for additional pretty, interactive invitation templates (greeting cards can be written out as invitations in the space where your message goes). There's a world of great designs out there!

~ Have the engagement party at home instead of at a reception hall or club. The comfortable, warm atmosphere is perfect for any level of formality. Just keep in mind that a home-based party of more than twenty or so guests will often mean added costs of rentals for extra tables, chairs, dishes, glasses, and other items. A smaller guest list often means you can use your own supply.

~ If you're planning on having the engagement party catered, cut costs a bit by having only part of the meal prepared by the professionals. They make the entrée, and you make the appetizers and desserts. You can easily cut a standard caterer's bill in half.

~ Plan the engagement party for a time during the day when no large meal will be expected. An informal affair from 2 to

5 P.M. is adequately served with hors d'oeuvres, and a soiree starting at 7 P.M. is best served with cake and dessert.

~ Shop for food and supplies in bulk or at a discount supply house like Costco or Sam's Club. These places offer great party-sized packages of frozen appetizers, deli trays, fresh seafood, and desserts for far less than regular or upscale markets. Have a friend take you on her membership if you don't belong to the club.

~ Cut down on beverage costs by limiting the variety of alcoholic and nonalcoholic drinks, or by choosing to serve only wine and beer.

DRINKS PORTION OF CATERER'S BILL
Events with alcohol . . . . $25–$30 more per person
Events without alcohol . . . . $15 more per person

~ A great resource for finding affordable, high-quality vintages, plus a unique assortment of recommended beers and liquors, is winespectator.com. Here you'll locate the best buys for your party.

~ Many brides report that they saved one hundred dollars or more by having a talented friend or relative make the cake or desserts for the engagement party. Many a grandmother has "donated" her time and ingredients for chocolate mousse, homemade cannoli, exotic fruit salad, or even an expertly decorated, butter-cream-frosted cake straight out of the pages of *Martha Stewart Living*. So if your cousin makes a sinful chocolate cheesecake, ask her to bring a few along as her present to you. With engagement presents costing fifty to one hundred dollars on the average, your cousin will secretly thank you for the giant savings. And she'll glow with pride when you announce to your guests that she is the pastry chef.

COMPARE AND SAVE
Store-bought sheet cake $75
Homemade sheet cake $20

~ Take your own pictures, and pass around the camera for help from family and friends. You may hire a professional photographer to take pictures at your engagement party, but you're trying to save money here, not waste it. This is just the engagement party, so informal, self-taken pictures will do fine. Use your own digital camera, not those ten to fifteen-dollar one-time-use cameras. That's just money wasted, once you add in the cost of developing them to see the shots everyone got.

COMPARE AND SAVE

Professional photographer . . . . $750 and up for one hour

Do it yourself . . . . $25–$50

∿ Instead of hiring a band, DJ, pianist, or harpist for your engagement party, turn on the stereo or your iPod dock if the engagement party is being held in your home, or have the restaurant or reception hall pipe in appropriate music through its sound system.

COMPARE AND SAVE

Professional music . . . . $650–$900

Stereo/piped-in music . . . . free

∿ As for decorations, consider a simple look. Fourteen dozen white balloons may look festive, but they're also a nonessential that can be thrown out in favor of saving some money. Create a classy look by decorating with vases of flowers cut fresh from your garden, well-placed pillar candles, or a display of photos of the two of you.

COMPARE AND SAVE

Balloons. . . . . up to $80

Vases of flowers from garden . . . . free

Display of photos . . . . free

~ You don't need to give out favors at the engagement party. Your guests won't expect them. But if you do want to give something out, inexpensive chocolates or sachets will do the trick.

~ Of course, you might choose not to have an engagement party at all. Many couples don't want to obligate their guests to travel. Just celebrate at a family holiday, such as Thanksgiving.

2

Your Wedding Planning Team

While many brides and grooms are marrying at older ages, once they're set in their careers and earning a solid paycheck and thus able to pay for their own wedding, many couples are welcoming the new trend of both sets of parents contributing money toward the big day. If this is you, keep these important money-saving tips in mind when it comes to parents chipping in.

~ These days, it's not just the parents of the bride who are paying for the wedding expenses. The parents of the groom are also getting in on the fun of planning and contributing an extra money source to the pool of wedding budget funds.

~ Grandparents are also giving brides and grooms a cash infusion to help offset the expensive costs of today's weddings.

Grandparents know that the wedding is a family day, as well as a day for the bride and groom, since many family members live so far apart.

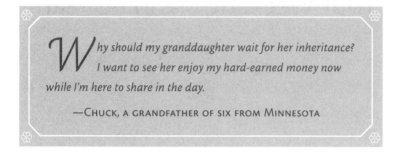

Why should my granddaughter wait for her inheritance? I want to see her enjoy my hard-earned money now while I'm here to share in the day.

—CHUCK, A GRANDFATHER OF SIX FROM MINNESOTA

∼ Keep the amounts that each set of parents are contributing a secret. At no time should either set of parents feel inferior to the other set because they have less money to give.

∼ Ask parents which areas of the wedding they'd like to pay for and help plan. It's always best to allow them to pick a category, like flowers, and play a part in decision making to accompany the money donation.

∼ Make sure that parents understand their financial donation doesn't mean they now "own" the wedding. Many parents create budget problems when they insist on a more formal wedding, pushing the bride and groom to make different choices and hire more upscale vendors so that they can impress their friends. When parents offer to help pay for the wedding, tell them their contribution will go a long way to help *your* wedding dreams and plans come true. If they ask to make the wedding larger, just say, "I wish we could, but that's not our wedding dream, and we don't want to go beyond anyone's original budget."

The Wedding Coordinator

~ A professional wedding coordinator can save you a ton of money by knowing which little-known sites fit into your budget and which vendors have the most experience at your style of wedding, at the best prices. These experts are a terrific source of savings, even if you do have to pay them a fee for their work.

~ You can hire a wedding coordinator just to help you find vendors, sites, and item resources for a few hundred dollars, instead of working your entire wedding at 15 percent of the cost of the wedding as a whole. You can get well-priced help-only packages for just a few hundred dollars . . . which can turn into a savings of thousands of dollars when the coordinator lands you the best-priced vendors.

∼ A wedding coordinator can save you a lot of money if you live in a different state from where the wedding will be held. Her in-town work means you don't have to make a lot of long-distance research phone calls.

∼ You can plan the wedding without the help of a wedding coordinator, especially if you have a team of volunteers who can recommend who they hired for their weddings or work on various wedding tasks. But ask yourself: is it worth the money savings to take on so much work?

∼ Ask a recently married friend to recommend the coordinator she used.

∼ Make sure the coordinator is a member of the Association of Bridal Consultants (bridalassn.com) or International Special Event Society (ises.com). Considering how much you'll be paying, it's best to make sure the person you hire is legitimate and well trained, with experience in your style of wedding.

∼ When you hire a wedding coordinator, carefully review the guidelines set up for your business relationship. Make sure you're both clear where your responsibilities begin and end, and don't hesitate to ask questions. It's your wedding.

3

Wedding Websites, Organizers, and Communication

Being organized is the number-one way to save money on your wedding. A disorganized approach can cost you extra money and time when a lost receipt means you have to pay a deposit again, a forgotten sale date means you miss out on a 70-percent-off discount, or a vendor mistakenly thinks you meant to double your order. You should take extra care to make sure you have a solid system in place for recording the details of your wedding plans. Likewise, you should also have a system in place for communicating with your wedding team, vendors, and guests so that they know deadlines, prices, and who's responsible for what. Being organized with your planning details will keep you stress-free and better able to make smarter spending decisions at each step of the planning process.

The Wedding Website

A personal wedding website is a great way to share links to the ceremony and reception sites, the hotel, and other points of interest. Your guests will appreciate having all of the important locations listed for them in one place.

~ A wedding website's list of locations and their websites means that guests can print out their own driving directions. You don't have to spend money copying directions or add extra weight to your invitation packets.

~ The wedding website can point your guests to local lounges, restaurants, and coffee shops so that you don't have to entertain them all weekend. You're giving them information to use when they have downtime on their own.

~ Check out weddingmapper.com, a free map-building site that allows you to input all of your important sites, from the wedding locations to your house to gas stations and other important places. Sending guests a link to your map means you don't have to print out maps for them!

∽ Check out at sites such as theknot.com for free wedding website setup, where you can choose your own colors and styles. Registries such as Bed Bath & Beyond also offer free personal wedding websites to registered brides and grooms.

Getting Organized

∽ Start planning and organizing early enough so that you have plenty of time to perform each job well. A rushed job means fewer chances to get more for your money, since you won't have time to comparison shop, ask questions, consider seasonal pricing, and visit holiday sales (a big source of budget items!). Nine months to a year is optimal for finding good deals at a savings. If short-term planning is required for a wedding that is less than a year away, do some research to find all of your professionals and locations without paying extra rush fees. Right now, wedding experts want your business, so they may eliminate rush fees. Be sure to ask about that.

∽ Encourage your mother, maid or matron of honor, bridesmaids, and friends to give you wedding planning books as their gifts to you.

BOOKS AND PLANNERS

Amazon.com—amazon.com

Barnes and Noble—bn.com

Borders—borders.com

↪ Use your local library's supply of gorgeous, color-photo coffee-table books written by celebrity wedding planners for planning inspiration, instead of spending sixty to seventy dollars to see the images within.

COMPARE AND SAVE

Bookstore wedding books . . . . $60–$70

Wedding book from library . . . . free

↪ Set up an organizer file using four-by-six-inch index cards and a recipe card file box. You've seen this suggested in all your bridal magazines and even in some ads for fifty-dollar index card and file-box sets with printed labels. Setting up a wedding planner file box of your own will work just as well, if not better.

⌇ You could also choose to turn an accordion file into your wedding organizer system. You'll find these in any office supply store for just a few dollars. Label each slot with a subject heading—Gown, Flowers, Music, Caterer—and filing brochures and swatches becomes simple.

⌇ Use your organization system to keep track of brochures, pictures, drawings, business cards, and all the important things that can get lost. The rule is, if you've lost it now, you'll need it later. And that can cost you money if something needs to be returned or an order needs to be placed.

⌇ Set up an organizer slot for receipts and contracts with "payment due" dates and "paid" stamps and dates. It's important to be able to show a vendor that you've already made a payment to avoid duplicate billing or late charges for not paying on time. You'll save a fortune by being able to prove you have paid. Many brides who lose their receipts are forced to pay twice.

⌇ Don't pay for expensive computer wedding planner programs. Do you really need your computer to remind you to go for your fitting at 4 P.M.? Besides, you can't file your brochures, swatches, and store receipts in the computer's files. While going high tech is a fun idea, it's also one of the worst cases of unnecessary wedding spending you'll ever see. Skip the software and stick with your own files, folders, or binder.

~ If you're set on having the computer help you out, use the free worksheets and tabulators at most of the top wedding planning websites, as well as at many bridal registry sections of home decor and department stores. It's now become a must for bridal sites to offer interactive planning tools online, for free.

WEDDING WEBSITES

The Best Man—thebestman.com

Bliss Weddings—blissweddings.com

Bride's Magazine—brides.com

Della Weddings—della.com

Destination Bride—destinationbride.com

Elegant Bride—elegantbride.com

The Knot—theknot.com

Martha Stewart Living—marthastewart.com

Modern Bride—modernbride.com

Pash Weddings—pashweddings.com

Premiere Bride—premierebride.com

Sharon Naylor Weddings—sharonnaylor.net

Today's Bride—todaysbride.com

Wedding Channel—weddingchannel.com

Wedding Details—weddingdetails.com

Wedding Solutions—weddingsolutions.com

Wedding Spot—weddingspot.com

⁓ Aside from wedding planning website worksheets, books, and articles, get yourself on track with the use of a handheld organizer such as your BlackBerry. You may already own one, so use it to create your wedding lists of to-dos, appointment reminders, and messaging centers.

⁓ Create your own organizational spreadsheets using Excel, where you can color-code your planning by category and use the program to add up columns for you. No doing math! Be sure to back up your files to a Zip disk or separate drive so that you don't lose your wedding plans if your computer crashes.

Communicating with Vendors

⁓ Don't rush into booking experts or making plans before you discuss them with your groom, your family, and anyone else who is involved. If they disagree with your decision, you can't get your money back, and you become an unreliable planning partner. It's not fair to rush ahead and make plans without others' input or permission. That's disaster to your budget, too. A hastily made decision can mean money lost when a contract has to be canceled or an item returned.

～ Get everything in writing. Written records can be referred to easily for reminders and deadlines, and oral contracts will not hold up in court in case of a problem. A written record of any business agreement should include the following details for clarification: date of sale; business's name and phone number; your name and phone number; date, time, and location of service; details of the service or items; delivery and payment arrangements; check number; cancellation or postponement policy; refund policy; and name and signature of the person who took the order.

GET IT IN WRITING

Tennessee-based attorney Karen Beyke advises, "Be sure your contract has a 'time is of the essence' clause, which states that a wedding provider must deliver the items or services at the proper time on the wedding day. Too many brides have complained that the flowers showed up at the church after the ceremony, or they had to wait an hour for the cake to be delivered from the bakery. If you have this phrase in your contract, the vendor will know you mean business, and you'll be sure to get timely treatment. If the item is not delivered on time, then they are in breach of contract, and you don't have to pay."

∽ Always get a copy of every contract and confirmation numbers from all the professionals who will be providing services during your ceremony or reception. This includes musicians, bakers, *everyone*. Never do business with any vendor who doesn't offer a written contract. You have to have proof of your agreements and payments.

∽ Read every word of your contacts, even if you have to sit back in your chair while the impatient salesclerk rolls his or her eyes and tries to hurry you along to the check-writing stage. You never know what's hidden in the fine print—extra charges, commissions, outlandish gratuities, special conditions, waivers, and so on. If you don't understand something in the contract, don't hesitate to ask.

∽ Just to be on the safe side, photocopy your contracts and keep the copies in a secure place. In case of loss, theft, or fire, you're still on secure ground with the larger expenses of your wedding.

∽ Get receipts for each of your deposits, signed and dated by the salesclerk. This way, you're preventing the old you-never-paid-me trick that some shadier companies might try on you.

PROFESSIONAL ASSOCIATIONS IN THE WEDDING INDUSTRY

American Disc Jockey Organization—adja.org

American Federation of Musicians—afm.org

American Rental Association—ararental.org

American Society of Travel Agents—astanet.com

National Association of Catering Executives—nace.net

Professional Photographers of America—ppa.com

Wedding and Portrait Photographers International—
eventphotographers.com

Keep in mind that your state may have its own associations for caterers, photographers, videographers, DJs, and so on, so do an Internet search for your own state's organizations where records might be kept on your prospective vendors.

∼ If you do wind up with a problem, go straight to the manager. No boss wants his or her business to get a bad report from an unhappy customer. Wedding industry professionals know that much of their business comes from referrals, and a bad reputation can slow down the flow of customers. The manager, you'll find, will be quick to fix the problem. If not, go to a consumer action group or consumer action column in your local paper (that'll get them hopping to please you), the Better Business Bureau, and the professional association affiliated with the business itself. To find your local chapter of the Better Business Bureau, log on to their site at bbb.org for company search instructions and report information. To check out an Internet company, contact the Better Business Bureau's BBB OnLine reliability program at bbbonline.org. These sites will assist in background searches on various companies you may be considering as vendors.

Keeping Yourself on Track

∼ Keep lists so you don't forget anything. Follow the lists provided in wedding books and magazines, or make up your own. (Ask the groom, the bridal party, and your families to do the same.)

∼ Keep several pads and pencils around the house, in your car, and at the office for when a thought or a question strikes you. Another rule of the wedding planner: if you think you'll remember it later, you won't. Write it down.

∼ If you're out on the town and inspiration strikes, call your home or cell number and leave a message for yourself on your own voice mail. Many brides do this when they pass a great bridal salon on the way to dinner or when someone recommends a great vendor.

~ One of your most important lists should be a price comparison list. Accounting ledgers are good for this job. You'll be able to assign each caterer, photographer, or band its own column, where you'll record prices and package details. Use this setup as you price all the services you'll need. A quick glance down a column on one piece of paper will reveal the choice with the best price and the most attractive offerings for that price. Highlight the best entries in each column. One bride who used this system found that she was better able to compare all the different packages, and in picking the best one she saved three hundred fifty dollars.

~ Keep a master list of phone numbers so you don't have to keep looking up important numbers or calling long-distance relatives for reminders of family members' phone numbers. When you feel organized, you feel more confident and wedding stress doesn't hit you as hard, forcing you into impulse buys and unwise purchases.

~ Record upcoming deadlines on both your home and work calendars, and record what you've already done as well. You may need to know exactly what day you ordered your gown so the salesperson can tell you if yours has arrived in the latest shipment. It's bad when you ask *them* when you paid. Some shady vendors may see you as disorganized and attempt to rip you off.

～ For each service you're arranging, call to confirm your order, delivery, and prices several times throughout the wedding planning months, most important a month before the wedding when your vendors will still have enough time to order something if they didn't get your order right the first time. With this much notice, you won't have to pay rush fees or accept a more expensive alternative plan or item.

It was a good thing I called to confirm. The florist said she had lost her appointment book in a robbery and she had no idea which weddings were planned for which days. She said it was lucky I called her. That's an understatement.

—STACY

～ Keep samples of fabric, ribbon, and lace and pictures of your gown and reception site in a box in your car so that you'll always have access to them when you're out shopping, at a big fabric sale, or in another city. Never guess at the color of your bridesmaids' dresses when you're out to buy coordinating items. A clash is a waste of money and shows your guests that you were unorganized and trying too hard to save some money.

~ Keep track of every wedding response you receive. Your final head count depends on those numbers, and it is that figure that tallies up one of the biggest expenses of your wedding: the catering. Keep your responses and a working yea-and-nay list in a large envelope or in your organizer, bound with a rubber band. Or use the small boxes your response cards and envelopes arrived in. Label the two boxes "Yes" and "No" and place each response card in the appropriate box. When guests call with a verbal RSVP, write their answer on a paper or card and slip that into the appropriate box as well for a 100 percent accurate head count to give to your caterer. The bulk of your wedding budget goes to the reception, so you need to be sure you have the right numbers for your adult and child guest counts.

*C*ommunicating with the *B*ridal *P*arty

A common situation facing more and more brides today is the problem of distance. Maybe it's because we're traveling more, meeting our men in places that bring people from distant parts together, and have computers that make it easier to carry on serious long-distance relationships. Whatever the reason, you'll still have to keep in contact with his and your families and friends who may be miles away during the planning stages of the wedding. Long-distance communication can cost money—a whole lot of it—so follow these steps for better, more economical long-distance organization.

〜 Know your phone company's off-rate hours and free weekend minutes, and plan to call team members or vendors then to save money on each call. At economy rates, the price per minute for your call could be half the regular rate. Some brides have saved up to two hundred dollars.

〜 Use e-mail not only as a fast and free way to communicate with your bridal party or vendors, but also as a record of when you sent messages out and when you received responses, as well as copies of everyone's information, sizes, confirmation that they paid, and so on. Save your messages into wedding folders, because many e-mail carriers now delete messages over three months old. Your e-mails will be safe in a folder.

〜 Send a copy of the wedding schedule to each member of the bridal party and to the families and friends who will be taking part in the wedding. This way, everyone is sure about what days to keep clear far in advance. Dates and times will not have to be shuffled at anyone's expense or aggravation.

〜 Ask the bridesmaids, maid or matron of honor, best man, and ushers to send you their measurements and sizes on index cards. With this information, you won't have to phone around to get them to admit their sizes when it's time to order their apparel. If shyness is a problem, have them send you their index cards in sealed envelopes to be opened only by the salesperson at the shop. Give them plenty of time to do this so no rush fees are incurred.

∼ Tell your attendants to have their sizes measured at a professional tailor's or seamstress's workshop; measurements taken with a tape measure or a piece of string and a ruler aren't nearly as accurate. One bridesmaid who took her own measurements with a tape measure misread her hip measurement and ordered the wrong size dress. When it arrived, it didn't fit, and she had to buy another dress on the double.

∼ To help your attendants and families stay organized—and to keep them from calling you all the time for one another's phone numbers—send out phone and e-mail lists of all the key players. You won't become the message-sender making long-distance calls. They can communicate on their own.

∼ If a bridal party or family member is slow in responding with important information, don't hesitate to explain how important it is to stay with the schedule. Apply some gentle pressure to get the job done. Or just use the broken record approach. Call the person up and say, "I don't remember if I've asked you this, but did you send me your size card already?" Of course, you know she didn't, but it doesn't hurt to play forgetful to get your point across.

4

Finding Savings at Bridal Shows

More than just a showcase of the talent available in your area, free drinks, and appetizers, the bridal show can lead you to extra discounts and even free honeymoons, gowns, and wedding day beauty treatments! Find out here how to make the most of your visits to bridal shows.

∽ Go to the bridal show to collect brochures, business cards, and prices (if they're available at the show) for your research. No need to travel all over town at great expense in time and gas money to all the bridal shops, shoe stores, caterers, florists, and photographers if each has information set up and available at the bridal show.

FINDING BRIDAL SHOWS

There are now many bridal show companies putting on wedding showcases in every town across the country and internationally. A great place to find the schedules and pricing for them is your local regional wedding magazine, such as New Jersey Bride *or* Connecticut Bride. *Just log on to their websites to find bridal shows planned for your area. One national company to check out is Great Bridal Expo, bridalexpo.com.*

~ Just use the show to get a sense of what you want from a three-dimensional representation of what you see in bridal magazines. The more exposure you get to real-life examples of wedding trends like cakes and invitations, the better able you'll be to make your own personalized decisions.

~ Some businesses set up at the bridal show may offer discounts to brides who sign up for their services on the spot. This takes away from your ability to comparison shop, so it may not be a good idea to go for the offer right away. Take time to check before you commit. You can always take their card and call them.

~ Attend both free and for-pay bridal shows to get acquainted with the widest range of wedding professionals in your area. Some vendors only showcase at expos where brides pay to attend, seeing those as "serious" brides and not those looking only for free food and champagne.

~ Door prizes are awarded at most bridal shows. They can range from silver frames to gift certificates for a wedding day makeover. Sign up for all giveaways. At a recent bridal show, one bride won a six-thousand-dollar Hawaiian honeymoon package and another won six free tuxedo rentals. Not bad for a twenty-dollar entrance fee. Any gift is money in your pocket. Speaking of gifts, you'll find samples of every kind at bridal shows. Makeup, perfumes, little portions of cake—all offered there for you to try without expense or obligation. So take advantage of these.

~ While you're there, see if there are any mailing lists you'd like to get on. Perhaps you'll be offered discounts. Just be prepared later for an onslaught of mail. The list you sign and the information you give may be sold to other retailers and businesses looking to attract your checkbook.

~ Play the games. The more creative vendors at the bridal event will have "try-your-luck" games such as a wheel of discounts that you can spin to win a percentage off their services or merchandise. Of course, these winnings are to be used only as incentives, not as your decision to hire that particular vendor. If the vendor checks out well during your comparison shopping, that 25-percent-off coupon will come in handy.

〜 Take the groom along with you so that he can check out all of the wedding planning options. Having him there saves time and money, as you won't miss out on offers because he's not around to share in the decision. If he needs a little prodding to attend one of these shows, just tell him there's free food, drinks, and entertainment.

〜 Participate in the show. Bridal shows often have mingling time during which you look at the booths. They also have an entertainment portion of the night when bands and DJs give performances to an admiring (and checkbook-holding) audience. If a DJ asks for a volunteer to come up on stage, either to take part in a conga line or simply sit there and be serenaded, you may want to raise your hand. Very often participants get a free gift or discount coupon.

〜 Talk to the experts to get ideas on how to save. While trying to win your booking, the pros will be very happy to chat with you as you ask about budget-cutting particulars for your wedding. For instance, a videographer may tell you more about editing costs, special effects fees, and efficient scheduling for the wedding day.

~ Stay until the end of the night. When the crowd clears out, some vendors make a practice of giving away their props to bridal-show attendees, rather than throwing them out or lugging them home. You might walk away with makeup samples, favors, and chocolates, even lovely silk centerpieces that can add to your wedding-day decor. One bride shared that the free silk centerpieces she got from a tired vendor made great decorations for the reception hall's restrooms. If she had ordered those from her florist she would have paid $250 for live arrangements.

~ Check the parking lot before you leave. Often the transportation companies bring a limousine, a stretch Navigator, even their decked-out party buses for prospective brides and grooms to see. One bride stepped into the party bus of a limousine company, heard the great sound system, saw the mood lighting and comfortable leather seats, and, after comparing costs for four limos for her bridal party, decided on the better buy—and the incredibly fun ride—of the party bus instead.

5

Your Gift List and Bridal Registries

You can save money with gifts other people give you, intended for wedding purchases, and by registering at the right places, at the right times, and for the right items. Too many brides cost themselves a big chunk of their gift money by leaving important items off their registry lists, having to buy necessities later. Here are the best ways to create your lists, plus some great registry sources.

Gift Lists

~ Ask for gift cards to craft stores, party supply stores, grocery stores, and beauty salons as your birthday and holiday gift suggestions to friends and family. You may have a year of gift-giving occasions to receive fifty to several hundred dollars worth of free purchases for your big day.

~ Ask your groom to give you gift cards for your beauty salon as an anniversary or birthday gift. Your wedding day hairstyle will be his gift to you, as well. The same goes for wedding night lingerie when he gives you a gift card to your favorite store.

Wedding Registries

~ Meet with an in-store bridal registry consultant before you begin filling out your choices online. She'll be able to answer your questions, direct you to resources you wouldn't have known about otherwise, and tell you about special messages and directions you can add to your registry file. Karen and Greg added this message to their registry file: "We prefer simple and elegant styles rather than busy or patterned styles." They received all appropriate items and saved themselves the hassle and expense of exchanges. Many stores also have free call-in gift registry specialists who can help you as well.

~ Obviously, it's smarter to register for things you need— like blankets, a coffeemaker, a microwave oven—than to fill your dream sheet with all those fun little extras and gadgets such as a shampoo dispenser for the shower or a personalized doormat. The idea is for the guests to help you set up your household, not to fill it with junk you'll have to clear out of the way for the new microwave you had to buy with your wedding money.

∼ The average bride and groom have two to three different bridal registries, giving them a wider range of gift possibilities. One top trend is registering at Home Depot or Lowes for home remodeling or design supplies, so that future purchases are taken care of without dipping into wedding gift money.

∼ Register for items in a wide range of expenses so that guests of all income levels have choices they can afford. Great ideas for inexpensive gifts include wines, books, CDs, kitchen gadgets, linens, and other items for less than twenty-five dollars.

∼ Register for a variety of gift card denominations on your online registry so that guests see that you want gift cards and can purchase one in their budget range. Many couples love getting gift cards because they can buy the items that weren't chosen on their registry, they can pool a number of gift certificates to the same department store to buy one big-ticket item, and they get a fun, guilt-free shopping spree.

WHERE TO REGISTER

Bed Bath & Beyond—bedbathandbeyond.com

Bloomingdale's—bloomingdales.com

Bon-Ton—bonton.com

Crate and Barrel—crateandbarrel.com

Della Weddings—dellaweddings.com

Dillard's—dillards.com

Eddie Bauer Home Collection—eddiebauer.com

Filene's—filenesweddings.com

Fortunoff—fortunoff.com

The Gift—thegift.com

Gift Emporia.com—giftemporia.com

Greenfeet (organic items)—greenfeet.com

Hecht's—hechts.com

Home Depot—homedepot.com

~ Let the maid or matron of honor and best man know what your much-wanted big-ticket item is, such as a home entertainment center, new computer, scanner, or mountain bikes. Your top attendants can consider pooling resources with the rest of the bridal party to get you an expensive item as their group wedding gift to you. This works as well with your parents. One couple expressed an interest in adding a room to their house, and the parents of the bride and groom joined forces to give them a check for that construction project as their wedding gift.

Honeyluna (honeymoon registry)—honeyluna.com

JCPenney—jcpenney.com

Kohl's—kohls.com

Linens 'n Things—lnt.com

Macy's—macys.com

Neiman Marcus—neimanmarcus.com

Pier 1 Imports—pier1.com

Sears—sears.com

Service Merchandise—servicemerchandise.com

Sharper Image—sharperimage.com

Sur La Table—surlatable.com

Target's Club Wedd Gift Registry—target.com

Tiffany—tiffany.com

The Wedding List—theweddinglist.com

Williams-Sonoma—williams-sonoma.com

∼ Check out honeymoon registries. Set up an account for a honeymoon fund and tell the honor attendants about the option of guests contributing to that fund, which can give you special tours, dinner cruises, romantic dinners, and spa treatments on your honeymoon—all without dipping into your wedding gift money! Warning: it is never appropriate to ask for money as a wedding present, so when you see home mortgage registries out there, know that they're not quite accepted by guests yet. Better to save your wedding gift money by signing on for a honeymoon list.

〜 If you're getting married at an older age, after you already have a fully stocked home and really don't want gifts, save your guests some money by asking them to donate their resources or time to their favorite charities in lieu of giving wedding presents to you. Two sources to check out are idofoundation .org and justgive.org.

〜 Let your friends and family know where you're registered through links on your personal wedding website, word of mouth, and inserts added to bridal shower invitations. It's considered rude to print your registry information in a wedding invitation.

〜 After you hand in your registry checklist, plan to get a printout of your registry as soon as it's entered into the computer. Search for and correct mistakes in your file right away so that no one buys you the wrong gift.

〜 Plan to update your registry after your engagement party, bridal showers, your own shopping trips throughout the months of planning, or whenever gifts are received to prevent receiving duplicates if people shop in a store without going through the registry system. Adding more gifts gives guests fresh choices, and you get 10 to 20 percent off on whatever's left on your list after the wedding through a "completion program" stores give you as an incentive to register with them.

⌘ Sorry, but you can't register for cash. Many brides have asked me about the etiquette rules for cash gifts, and I'm sorry to report that your guests will have to make up their own minds as to whether to give you a check. Do not rationalize that if you do not register, then your guests will automatically give you cash gifts. What you're more likely to get is the guest's idea of the perfect present, which could be his-and-hers cow-shaped milk dispensers for morning coffee. (Don't laugh—it has happened.)

⌘ After your wedding, let friends and family know that your registry will be online for a year as a list for future birthday and holiday gifts.

⌘ Do you have insurance for your wedding gifts? The expense is worth it.

⌘ Arrange for someone, perhaps your parents, to take your wedding gifts to their home after the reception for safekeeping while you're away. This is one of the best forms of insurance known. Never leave your house empty and full of new and valuable merchandise.

6

Your Bridal Party

Before you bestow the honors upon your closest friends and relatives, read this chapter for budget issues that arise in selecting your bridal party. Don't forget that being an honor attendant will cost your chosen few a pretty penny, so look for ways to help them save cash as well.

⌁ Choose a smaller bridal party, perhaps limited to sisters and brothers. After all, if you have eight bridesmaids and eight ushers plus flower girls and ring bearers, you'll have to pay for that many gifts, perhaps arrange lodging for all of them, rent more limos, and so on. Not only is a smaller bridal party a savings for you, it will also prevent headaches over which of your cousins, friends, and coworkers to include in the lineup. One bride estimated her expenses per attendant—including gifts, planning luncheons, and apparel (her choice)—to be $175.

Others estimated their per-attendant amount in the fifty-to-seventy-five-dollar range.

∼ Consider just having a maid or matron of honor and a best man as your bridal party. Male relatives can act as ushers to seat the guests.

∼ Just have flower girls. It's a charming look. Beverly was able to outfit and buy gifts for her six flower girls for the cost of one designer-style bridesmaid's dress.

∼ Rather than having to choose a few friends out of a handful of special ones, choose none. The same goes for your twelve first cousins. It sounds harsh, but you can explain that you love them all and didn't want to leave anyone out.

∼ When you choose your bridal party, particularly the maid or matron of honor and best man, be sure you can depend on the people you're involving. Maturity and dependability are important. You don't want to include disinterested people who aren't able to keep appointments and deadlines because a big party just came up or something really good was on television. Remember, your bridal party is more than just a collection of well-dressed men and women; the position has meaning and purpose. You don't want to have to spend your time and money backtracking on the responsibilities of your attendants.

~ Don't be pressured to choose people based on their standing in the family in general (such as all cousins). Your honor attendants should be individually special to you.

~ Don't include obviously bitter, jealous, or unsupportive attendants or ushers out of a sense of responsibility. These people will be impossible to work with, and they'll put a damper on your day. Plus, you may find yourself paying for the uncooperative person's gown, tux, or other items just to get it done, or to avoid a confrontation.

~ Don't include someone just because you were in her bridal party years ago. You should not use your wedding to "pay back" people.

~ The best way to save money on your bridal party is to keep them updated on your decisions, supply them with lists of their responsibilities and deadlines, and be receptive to their input throughout. People management is a smart way to save yourself extra trouble and expense.

〜 Don't offer to pay for their wardrobe or travel, especially at the start of the wedding plans when you're excited and not yet fully into your wedding purchases. Some well-meaning brides make the grand gesture, which is wonderful if you have an endless budget. But making a big offer like this can lead to big expenses. You can't take back the offer later, because some bridal party members may have agreed to be in the party because you volunteered to take on some of the financial burden.

〜 If your bridal party is traveling into town for the wedding, save a few bucks by getting them booked in your discount room block, offering a range of nearby hotels in moderate price ranges, or suggesting a quaint bed-and-breakfast for less than a hotel room price (visit bnbfinder.com to locate bed-and-breakfasts near your wedding location). Think twice about letting bridal party members stay at your place unless you truly do have extra bedrooms. You'll have a lot to do during the days before the wedding, and you won't want to entertain houseguests when you're supposed to be focused on the wedding.

〜 Try to find ways to save them money. Choose inexpensive designers for their gowns and tuxes. Give them their accessories as gifts. Don't pressure them to join you at boot camp. Don't require them to get their hair and makeup professionally done unless they want to. Hint that you'd prefer a more casual shower, not high tea at a fancy hotel. Let them know that you care about their expenses and that you don't want to burden them with exorbitant price tags. I hear too many stories about bitter bridesmaids who resent the bride for being too self-focused and demanding with expenses. Your bridal party should enjoy this time, not dread every phone call from you about another fifty dollars they have to shell out.

7

Setting a Budget

I know, I know. Setting a budget is about as much fun as serving jury duty, but it's a vital part of planning a wedding efficiently and frugally. It's important to keep in mind that a budget can be adjusted during the course of your planning to reflect your true wants and needs, so you don't have to begin this task with dread. Many brides I've spoken to report that they loved beating the numbers in their budgets by finding great deals and shifting the extra money into other areas of their wedding expenses. Learn here how to create a workable budget for the wedding of your dreams.

〜 Before you sit down to create your wedding budget, research the prices of basic wedding services in your area. That way, your budget will be more realistic. Visit costofwedding .com to see survey results on the averages spent in your area when you enter your zip code. Knowing the ballpark figures will help you create a more realistic budget.

∾ List every single expense you will have to face. Start with the obvious ones, and then look through magazines and ask married friends about all those hidden extras like delivery charges. To cheer yourself up, list what you can get for free.

∾ Then make another list of the top three or four things on which you'll spare no expense—or at least not scrimp on too much. These may be your gown, the catering, your honeymoon—whatever you feel most strongly about. With these items arranged, you'll be better able to find the right places to cut spending.

∾ Add to your list of expenses a reserve for any miscellaneous spending that may come up, such as taxes, tips, and transport fees, so you won't chip away at the main budget with all the little things.

∾ Look at your available cash flow to see where you stand. Designate a percentage of your savings and projected income until the wedding date to determine your wedding funds. You don't want to throw yourself far into debt with loans or a drain on your credit cards, and you don't want to sell your prized possessions to dig yourself out of the hole after the big day. Don't plan to spend the amount you expect in wedding checks, because very few brides and grooms receive their projected gift money amounts from guests. Then they're in trouble because they counted on it (and pre-spent it!). It's better to stick with what you have than to overextend yourselves.

~ Decide how the expenses will be divided. What will your parents be able and willing to finance? The groom's parents? What will you foot the bill for? This list will take some work, as money can be a highly sensitive issue to everyone involved in planning a wedding. Foster a sense of cooperation and compromise. Full input by all is recommended so that no one feels as if they've been unfairly assigned an expenditure, and if both sets of parents want to work on the cake they can work on it together. The result will be a smart outline for the handling of your wedding budget. Put each parent's task in writing on a spreadsheet and share it with everyone to avoid future confusion or double purchases.

~ Try to save money for everyone involved. Bear in mind your families' and friends' cash flows when you make decisions that will affect them, and they in turn will try to help save money for you as well.

⌒ Be sensitive if one family is in a higher income bracket than the other. It's unfair to burden one with the job of keeping up with the other. Keep expenses for both groups even so neither family feels it is doing more than the other. Nothing fosters family tensions faster than money problems.

⌒ Don't push expenses off on to your families. Not only is it inconsiderate to ask too much, you could be handing over a certain amount of control over your decisions as well. What bride hasn't heard, "I'm paying for this, am I not?"

⌒ Keep a working record of your expenses as you go along. It's best to keep on top of the flow of checks and bills. Carry a small notepad with you for recording purchases, and carry an envelope in which you'll store receipts.

⌒ Use a computer finance program such as Quicken or Microsoft Money to keep track of your wedding expenses. These programs will categorize your expenses, let you know what the totals are in each category, alert you to bill due dates, and help keep you on budget by giving you a clear, organized picture of the checks you're writing and the charges you're making. Most standard computers come with these programs, so you might not need to spend extra on them.

~ Don't become a slave to the magic number. Your budget is just a framework to keep your spending under control. If the flowers actually cost you sixty-five dollars more than you'd expected, don't cut the grandmothers' corsages just to slide under the limit. Most brides believe they lost control of their spending (not to mention their temper) when they felt most constrained by the budget they'd arranged months ago.

~ If you think the budget might turn into additional pressure for you (perhaps you've had experience with budgeting before), set your limits slightly higher than you'd like them to be. An extra twenty dollars tacked on to each projected expenditure could make you feel triumphant instead of guilty when you sign the photographer's contract for five dollars under your budget. (Sure, it's a game you play with yourself, but it's important to downplay the significance of the money so that you don't start to feel it's controlling your wedding.)

~ Know the difference between price and value. Always think of what you're getting in terms of quality. Never, ever choose the least expensive option because you'll always be disappointed. Find a happy medium between price and product and make your decisions based on value.

~ Price items and services on the Internet, over the phone, and through in-store research to get a good idea of the going rates before you set your budget. Don't guess, and don't simply ask others what they paid for their flowers. Send for free brochures, call for price lists, look at local vendor guides on the supermarket shelf and in bookstores. Creating a realistic budget using the current numbers in the market is the best way to save money in the long run.

~ Talk to a wedding consultant for a free initial consultation to see if he or she can help shave money from your budget.

~ Practice your bargaining skills. I always advise brides and grooms to try to negotiate discounts and free items on volume purchases. Negotiation takes a little practice and a lot of self-confidence, but it's the best way to get the most for your money. It sounds odd, but to hone your skills, visit a flea market in town. That's where real haggling takes place, and you may perfect your skills before trying your hand at the wedding vendors.

~ If you do arrange a service for well below the amount you originally budgeted for it, exercise great control by not blowing the amount you saved on something trivial. Instead, enter that amount in a reserve that will allow you to slip slightly over budget in another category . . . like your gown.

~ Decrease the number of guests if you need to cut expenses. Just don't try this after the invitations have been sent. You can't uninvite a person.

~ Lower the formality of the wedding if your introductory research indicates that a formal dinner reception will be too expensive. Choose an alternative that is more economical, such as a luncheon or a tea party.

Caterer's Prices

Full dinner for fifty .... $100–$200 per guest

Luncheon for fifty .... $70–$100 per guest

Tea party for fifty .... $30–$50 per guest

~ Try the age-old barter system. See if you can trade your professional services for free or discounted vendor contracts. You might be able to talk the vendor into giving you a percentage off services in exchange for an hour of your time as a professional office organizer or as an artist who can stencil a border in his or her shop.

∽ What about getting services for free in exchange for advertising the vendor's product? Much has been written about "sponsored weddings" in the wedding industry, with some couples even going on television to rave about how they got their entire weddings for free by emblazoning their wedding programs with such notations as "flowers provided by . . . ." While you might be able to arrange for such free services, be smart about your choices and don't turn your wedding into the Super Bowl. We're attacked by advertising twenty-four hours a day, and your guests may find it tacky to have business cards and media kits at their table place settings. Choose wisely and advertise subtly if you use this tactic. Perhaps your florist will allow you to simply set a pretty box of their business cards next to a floral arrangement in the reception hall's main room.

8

Timing Your Wedding

Timing is everything, and the thirty-two-billion-dollar wedding industry puts a price tag on all of its offerings according to supply and demand at various times of the year. Choosing the right date for your wedding could save you a bundle!

The Season

~ First, allow yourself plenty of time to consider several seasons for your wedding. This might mean up to a year of waiting and planning, but you can save a lot of money with careful research in this area. For instance, a spring wedding date might cost one-third as much as the identical wedding held in late summer! Wedding sites and vendors price according to their busy season, and when they want to attract more winter or spring weddings to book more events, they drop their prices in these off-peak times.

∽ Know when peak season is in your region of the country. You've read that the time when weddings are most expensive is between May and September, but that's not always true in all areas of the country. Where you live, it might be 75 degrees year-round, so November could be peak season. Talk to wedding coordinators and wedding vendors to find out the best-priced months in your area.

∽ Think about the style of wedding you would want at a spring wedding, a summer wedding, a fall wedding, or a winter wedding. Would an outdoor wedding in the fall require lots of rentals? Would you be happy with an indoor wedding during the winter? Right now, it's easy to envision which extra expenses you might incur, without actually knowing the hard statistics. Just thinking about a mountain of rentals for your summer outdoor wedding might convince you to take it inside during the late fall months.

∽ Looking at the national survey results at theweddingreport.com, the most popular months for weddings (and therefore the months when supply and demand sometimes mean that prices will be higher) are June, August, and September, with May, July, and October following close behind. So, for the best availability and rates—and according to some brides, better service from unhurried vendors—consider planning your wedding during January through April or in November or December (excluding holiday weekends in these two months, when rates spike). Of course, always compare prices for any date you choose. Making the right selections in your wedding purchases by using this book, you may be able to put together an inexpensive fete smack in the middle of June.

Nonpeak Months

The survey on theweddingreport.com shows the most popular— or peak—wedding months are May through September. The most popular nonpeak months, in order of demand from most to least, are as follows:

November

April

March

December

February

January

Weather and Travel Issues

∼ The season of your wedding may determine if you'll have weather factors to consider. Are you planning an outdoor wedding during the rainy season? If so, when you have to move everyone and everything indoors to a booked party room as your Plan B, the garden tea party that was much less expensive than a sit-down dinner will wind up costing you much more than you had planned. You can't predict the weather because it can be cold on Memorial Day and hot in April, so take weather into consideration if you're planning a wedding in the elements.

∼ Will it be the stormy time of year where you're planning to spend your honeymoon? A great deal of money will be wasted if you lose a day or two of your vacation because a flight was delayed by a hurricane. So consider the seasonal weather when you plan your wedding and honeymoon.

∼ The travel industry is also controlled by seasonal rates. Off-season airfare and hotel reservations can amount to hundreds of dollars in savings compared to high-season tourist prices. Check with your travel agent about seasonal travel prices when you begin your planning, or check directly with airlines, hotels, and tourism boards. This applies to travel you'll do for the wedding, not just the honeymoon!

∾ Holidays also affect the price of travel for the bride and groom and for family and friends who will come from miles away to share your day with you. Either travel and lodging fees will soar skyward due to holiday visiting, or special holiday travel packages may be offered to lure customers away from competitors. Research holiday travel rates thoroughly before you plunk down a few thousand on Labor Day weekend. You might be able to get a better deal at another time.

∾ Another way to facilitate travel: plan your wedding for the weekend of a family gathering or reunion. Everyone will be in the general area, and they'll get two great events for one trip. One bride found that when she moved her wedding date to an earlier weekend, more of her guests would be in the area after a family party, and she saved more than a thousand dollars in travel and lodging for her guests. Although this should never be your motivation, you may find that grateful guests will be slightly more generous with their wedding gifts to you.

∾ The season of your wedding will also affect the price of the flowers you choose for your bouquets and decorations. Blooms and plants are usually cheaper when they're in season, so consider your florist bill when you set a date. (More on flowers in Chapter 21.) Furthermore, a wedding planned for Valentine's Day faces an increased charge for much-in-demand roses. Eighty-dollar bouquets on Valentine's Day go for less than twenty dollars the day after, so imagine what your wedding flowers will cost.

~ Prices and types of food on the wedding menu will also be affected by the season. Warmer days mean lighter, simpler foods, and certain types of seafood, meats, and produce are less expensive when in season. Talk to your caterer for information about which food items are best priced during which seasons, and look at Chapter 28 for more information on budget food choices and timing tricks.

Wedding Dates to Avoid

To avoid high prices, stay away from the popular holiday wedding dates, such as New Year's Eve and Valentine's Day. For all the glory of sentimentality, you'll pay a very high price. Some establishments, for instance, charge triple for New Year's Eve weddings.

One bride confides that you also should not plan your wedding too close to tax season, the week before April fifteenth and shortly thereafter. "Everyone was so stressed out about the taxes they owed, they couldn't travel or give us the kinds of gifts they would have otherwise been able to give," she says. So if you're in a high tax bracket, skip the middle of April.

$\mathcal{D}$ay of the Week

 Reconsider a Saturday-night gala event. It is still pretty much the norm for brides and grooms to have their weddings on a Saturday, so that is the day of the week that is most highly booked and most expensive. You can however still book that Saturday wedding for 30 to 40 percent off just by choosing the earlier time slot for an afternoon wedding—such as noon to five o'clock in the evening—as the first wedding that site will host that day (when their chefs and servers have more energy to give you top-notch service!). Saturday may actually turn into the best decision possible!

 Or look at a Friday night or Sunday afternoon wedding. These alternative days are usually less expensive by 20 to 30 percent, more easily booked, and offer great alternatives to the standard Saturday night sit-down dinner at $150 a head. A late Friday night reception may be a champagne and dessert event at 9 P.M., or a Sunday afternoon event may be an outdoor wedding on the beach. So consider it now while the wedding industry still considers these days "off days" and does not charge more for them. As time goes by, they will become standard, and there will be no price difference.

~ One new trend is holding the wedding on a Thursday night if all of your guests live in town or within a half-hour's drive. Thursday night catering prices can be 50 percent off weekend pricing!

Time of Day

The clock decides not only the formality of your event but also the expenses that go along with it. Use this chapter to decide if you and your fiancé are going to be morning people or night people.

~ Wedding sites charge different rates for different times of the day, depending on the style of meal you serve, so it is usually less expensive to have the ceremony in the morning than in the afternoon or evening. When researching ceremony locations, look through price brochures or ask questions to find out if your choice has a time factor in the fees.

~ According to wedding tradition and etiquette standards, the time of day of the wedding and reception determines the degree of formality. A morning wedding and brunch will cost nowhere near the total for the ultraformal candlelight ceremony and 8 P.M. sit-down dinner affair. So when choosing a time to reserve the ceremony site and reception hall, consider the festivities appropriate to that time of day. If you're going by etiquette rules, 8 P.M. is traditionally the time for a very formal dinner.

Average Meal Cost

Breakfast weddings . . . . $30 per person

Brunch weddings . . . . $30–$40 per person

Luncheon weddings. . . . . $40–$50 per person

High tea (3 or 4 P.M.). . . . . $20–$30 per person

Cocktail party (4 or 5 P.M.). . . . . $40–$70 per person

Dinner (5 to 8 P.M.) . . . . $60–$150 per person

Late night (9 P.M. and later). . . . . $60 and up (late-night parties often mean more alcohol)

∽ Beyond formality, it's simply less expensive to serve your guests a wonderful range of hors d'oeuvres at 1 P.M. than filet mignon at 9 P.M. Plan your menu according to time of day for greater savings. Done properly, offering hors d'oeuvres can be every bit as classy as the full meal arrangement. More so, perhaps, depending on your choices and presentation.

∽ Another plus for the earlier reception: it's easier to get away with having an economical nonalcoholic reception earlier in the afternoon than it is at night. Many families host traditional nonalcoholic receptions due to their belief systems, and the bride and groom may decide to adhere to this plan as a way to honor familial values and save a fortune on the reception. Guests are more apt to accept the "rule" in the afternoon than in the evening. No mutiny at the bar.

∽ Consider the weather. If you plan an outdoor wedding for the hottest part of the day, your roses will wilt and your cake may slide off the table. It has happened. The weather becomes a factor in your expenses, or—more likely—in wasted expenses on the big day. Check out the average weather conditions for your wedding date and time and make your decisions accordingly. A three o'clock wedding will get you all out of the peak sun, spare your menu items, and be more comfortable for all.

∽ The time of day may affect traffic patterns in your area and on the roads leading to your area. Arrival times for guests, the officiant, your flowers, your cake, and even yourself may be affected if major logjams occur on the highways near your site. This is especially true if you've planned your wedding for a holiday weekend. Rather than allowing the traffic to adversely affect your day, you can save money in wasted fees and delays by figuring travel times into your delivery and travel schedules.

～ Be careful of extra charges related to the time of day of your wedding. Some locations and companies will charge you extra for a late-night wedding if they cannot get in to clean up or break down items until the next morning. That means an extra day's rental fees. An earlier wedding means your guests will be gone by 7 or 8 P.M., and the items can be returned on the same day. Ask if the rental agency will waive the extra day's fee because your event is at night (most will—all you have to do is ask!).

～ Think of your guests' schedules. A Friday-night wedding scheduled to start at 6 P.M. may mean that many of your guests will not be able to get to the ceremony or the cocktail hour in time because of their work schedules and travel times. Even if they don't show up until well into the reception, you've still paid their per-head fees for the cocktail hour. The best way to avoid such wasted money is to have a Friday night wedding at 8 P.M. (which makes it a formal event) or have a Sunday event in the morning to afternoon hours so that everyone has time to travel home.

9

Your Guest List

Size does matter when it comes to per-guest expenses. Everything from the location to the meals and drinks served depends on the head count of your guests. There's no need to try to save money by slicing your guest list to pieces and alienating half of the people you know. With some smart planning you can work your guest list to give you the opportunity to spend less on your wedding while still including many friends, relatives, and colleagues.

~ Make it clear to your parents that the guest limits for each side are firm numbers so that neither side overextends, thinking they can just slide by. Make it known how serious you are about the ten to twenty friends you allowed them to invite, and you'll avoid the tensions of overstepped boundaries. Too many brides have been pushed into accepting "just three more" over and over—and at $50 to $150 per person, the figures add up.

~ Ask parents not to mention the wedding to their colleagues and friends until you're 100 percent sure of your final guest count . . . which may need to be cut down when the budget gets strained by wedding expenses. Since you can't uninvited a person, it's better to limit parents' chatting—which can lead to extra invitations.

Average Number of Guests

According to theweddingreport.com, the average number of wedding guests nationwide is 166. While most weddings include between one hundred and two hundred guests, a half million weddings per year include more than two hundred guests.

~ Organize your potential wedding guests into groups, such as first cousins, second cousins, best friends, closest colleagues. You'll then list these groups by tiers, such as (1) immediate family, (2) best friends, (3) aunts and uncles, (4) first cousins, (5) college friends, (6) bosses and closest colleagues, (7) second cousins, (8) family friends, (9) distant colleagues, and (10) parents' friends we don't know. With this visual "hierarchy" of your guests, you can more easily cut entire groups from the bottom up, starting with parents' friends you don't know and the entire pack of distant colleagues you rarely talk to.

∼ If you have to invite many guests, plan a more informal reception to reduce the cost of meals per person. This could mean fifty dollars less per person when you plan a high tea rather than a sit-down dinner for your big guest list.

∼ A four-hundred-plus-person guest list often sends couples to the concept of a destination wedding with twenty or so guests in attendance. If you choose to skip the gigantic wedding for a destination wedding at a fraction of the cost, you can still have an informal party for your extended family and friends to attend when you get home from the honeymoon. This post-party can cost one-tenth the price of a formal wedding!

∼ Don't attempt to "beat the wedding budget" by making your guest list too small. You'll insult relatives and friends by excluding them, and you'll also feel that you've ripped yourself off when there's next to nobody passing through the receiving line. Just work toward a fair and comfortable medium.

～ Make sure your guest head count works with the size of your ceremony and reception sites before you send out invitations or verbally invite people. Each site has a fire-safety maximum capacity, which you cannot exceed. Going overboard will mean you have to book a different site, lose deposits, perhaps reprint invitations and maps, and so on.

$\mathcal{K}$*ids and Teens*

～ Consider excluding children. With the wording of your invitation, you can indicate to your guests that their children are not invited to the wedding.

～ Ask your site manager or caterer if kids eat free. Many sites welcome all-family weddings by not charging anything for kids under age ten to attend the reception. This means you don't have to pay for kids' meals, nor for a babysitter for off-site child care.

～ Ask the site manager what they charge for kids' meals. If they charge half the price of an adult meal for kids ages three through twelve, that may still be too much money to spend. Will a five-year-old really eat forty dollars worth of food? *You* probably won't eat forty dollars worth of food that day!

Take kids' meal prices into consideration when building your guest list.

∽ If guests write on their response cards that they're bringing their kids when you didn't invite the little ones, it's a *must* for you to call the parents and explain that you can't invite kids for space and budget reasons. Don't get bullied into allowing some kids to attend, or *all* kids will attend.

∽ If you can't foot the bill for a babysitter for guests' kids (as some wedding couples do), suggest that guests bring their own babysitter or another relative along for the trip. The sitter or grandparent stays with the kids, and then the family gets a hotel stay on the wedding weekend.

∽ Teenagers don't need to bring a date or a friend to the wedding. Yes, they would feel more comfortable if their crush was there but not at a hundred dollars per person.

"And Guests"

∽ Etiquette-wise, all single guests older than age eighteen should get an "and guest" invitation. But if you're tight on budget, you might not want to double your guest list this way. Just explain to guests that you wish you could extend plus-ones to everyone, but you had to cut a lot of relatives out of your wedding day since your guest list has grown too big. Good friends will understand that they can't bring a rent-a-date to this one.

~ If guests have significant others, it's best to allow them to bring their dates. Some wedding guides say "limit it to engaged guests only," but that just angers guests. It's far better to extend the "and guest" to all and find other ways to save money.

~ A little trick: have several of your single friends spread the word that they're not bringing rent-a-dates. The trend of going solo to a wedding is picking up, since weddings are a great place for singles to meet. No one wants to babysit a boring date all night, so have friends talk about the virtues of not bringing a guest even though they were granted ones.

~ "And guest" status will be evident in the wording of the invitation, but if a person who has not received an "and guest" invitation indicates to you that she's planning to bring a date, it's your right to remind her that space limitations prevent you from letting her bring a guest. Tell her how your sister, the maid of honor, isn't even bringing a guest. If a response card is returned to you with a written-in addition of a guest's escort (an entirely inappropriate move if not cleared with you first), call the offender and tactfully remind him or her that space on the guest list does not allow additional people to be invited to the wedding. Don't be manipulated into paying for this extra person when your college roommates, your boss, and your second cousins all had to be left off the list.

~ When looking at price per head, keep in mind that you will have to feed the entertainment. A DJ is only one person and only one meal, while a full band may cost you twelve full meals. It's best to keep the numbers low. Also on the "feed" list: the photographer, videographer, and wedding coordinator. Even with caterer's "vendor meals" at twenty-five dollars per person, that adds up!

Cutting the List Down

~ When expenses look like they could start getting out of hand, it's time to start cutting the guest list. Begin with the bottom tiers and work your way up. It makes it easier on you when you can tell relatives you had to draw the line at first cousins due to space and budget issues. This boundary keeps you from overinviting and spares hurt feelings. You had a fair plan, and you stuck with it!

⌒ Cut those guests who have drifted from you in the past few months and years. This can be hard to do, but it's a relief to just close the door on friends you've outgrown.

⌒ Cut old high school and college friends you're sure you'll never see again.

⌒ Cut people you're inviting simply because you were invited to their wedding fifteen years ago, but you haven't seen or spoken to more than three times since.

⌒ Cut your parents' friends and clients who don't really know you. Of course, make sure your parents are aware of your decision to prevent any conflicts or hurt feelings.

⌒ Cut out any work friends with whom you never socialize outside of the office. Make that your dividing line so that you don't get stuck inviting forty extra people out of a sense of obligation, who then feel obligated to attend. (It is good form, though, to invite your bosses, especially if they cut you some slack at the office while you were planning the wedding.)

⌒ Don't send invitations to faraway relatives to be nice with the idea that they won't be able to make it. They might decide to hop a plane and attend after all; then you have to add on a handful of guests you hadn't counted on. One bride was shocked when overseas relatives responded that all ten of them would attend her wedding. Her advice: "Be careful whom you invite; they just may show up."

∽ It's no longer the responsibility of the bride's family to pay for out-of-town guests' travel and lodging. Times have changed, and they pay for their own! This is an important factor when building your guest list.

Make People Your Priority
People make the wedding memorable. Not the flowers or the dress or the cake.

10

Your Ceremony Location

Where you hold your wedding is almost as important financially as the type of wedding you plan. Certain locations obviously cost more, but some bring extra expenses you may not be aware of. Use this chapter to select the most cost-efficient location for your big event and to find ways to save once you book it.

~ Of course, your church, synagogue, or other place of worship may be the obvious choice for reasons other than the minimal expense of reserving it for your ceremony. Most establishments just ask for a donation and an officiant's fee, and that is still much better than a thousand-dollar location rental bill.

~ Meet with your officiant about scheduling and restrictions. Before you make any plans or put down any deposits, you'll need to know if there are rules about which musical selections and performers you can arrange and whether or not photographers are allowed. If, for instance, you find that your church does not allow harp music during wedding ceremonies, you will lose the deposit you already gave to the harpist.

~ Be up-front about any special information the officiant should know. Attempting to hide such things as your different religions is a very bad idea. You could find your ceremony canceled on you if your officiant is strict about limits.

Your Search for a Location

~ Look around far in advance. Most churches and synagogues are booked up to a year or two in advance. Looking early can get you in the door or give you a head start in looking for alternate locations that match the formality of the wedding.

~ Make sure the location is suitable for your religion(s). Some religious officiants will not conduct rites in certain secular locations or outdoors. Ask the officiant to review the site and give you written approval for it.

~ Make sure the location is suitable for the number of guests who will be attending your ceremony. A chapel that's too large will make your wedding look barely attended. A setting that's too small will cause grumbling over standing-room-only or too-hot conditions.

~ Make sure the location offers the necessary facilities: restrooms, electricity, parking, handicapped access, and so on.

~ Will it be necessary to rent chairs and other items in order to use this location for the ceremony? It could turn out to be an expensive proposition, as chair rentals can reach into the hundreds of dollars. It's best to book a site that offers comfortable and adequate seating.

~ Make sure you will be allowed enough time in that location for the completion of your ceremony. You don't want to be rushed out of the place so the next wedding can begin.

~ Will your deposit be returned if you decide against this location? Ask if there's a time limit, such as six months before the wedding, when you can get a refund.

Outdoor Settings

∾ A wedding on the beach is still one of the most romantic choices available to you. For the nominal price of an official license to gather in the oceanside spot you choose and various permissions that are more legwork than check-work, you have available to you a priceless wedding location. Other options include a park, lake, or beautiful garden.

∾ Try your county's arboretum. For a comfortable fee you'll have access to a banquet hall, a gazebo, and tons of beautiful flowers and floral backdrops for great pictures. Many arboretums feature ponds, brooks, waterfalls, and fountains, all a built-in part of this location that will save thousands on your floral bill.

∾ Some locations offer the free services of their own wedding coordinators. These well-studied professionals can save you additional money by advising on what's allowed and not allowed at the site, whether the site will already be decorated for the holidays or other special events, and which vendors work at a discount through them.

∾ Another inexpensive setting more suitable to the informal or semiformal wedding is a field of flowers. Nothing approaches the beauty of nature more closely than the beauty of matrimony. Again, though, all that beauty may still require a license from your town. Drinking in public and gathering after dark may be against the public order in some regions. A quick check can save you a fortune in tickets.

~ If you're considering an outdoor setting, be sure to add in the weather factor. You may have to move if it begins to rain. And if you miss the rainstorm, you'll still have mud to contend with.

~ Most outdoor ceremony sites require permits for their use. Be sure to ask the main offices of state parks, arboretums, even your local town hall if you plan to hold the ceremony on your own front lawn. Different cities have different rules about large gatherings. Permits are often not expensive, but getting a ticket for *not* having one can cost hundreds of dollars. It's better to ask first.

~ Outdoor ceremony sites require chairs and perhaps a tent. Ask if your chosen site offers these for free (many do), or if you'll need to pay for rentals.

~ Ask your site if they charge per person for ceremony attendance. Some sites, such as gardens where your reception may be held, charge a nominal fee of two to five dollars per person to cover the expense of using the site's chairs, staff setup and cleanup, and so on. Be sure to factor this per-person charge into your budget.

Additional Settings

∽ Some economical settings to rent for your ceremony include a restaurant, service-club hall, gallery, social or country club, community center, museum, or aquarium.

∽ Bed-and-breakfasts are growing in popularity as the site for ceremonies and receptions, usually at great savings over catering halls. Visit bnbfinder.com to find a B&B near you.

∽ Have your wedding at a mansion. Check with your local historical society for details, and you'll find a variety of gorgeous homes with some historical significance open to you as a setting for your day. Either hold the festivities indoors, perhaps in the grand dining room, or make use of the mansion's garden and gazebo.

∽ Check with your local historical society for other ideas for free wedding locations. They may be able to direct you to a wonderful and noteworthy spot you'll love.

~ Consider a winery for an intimate gathering. Many brides find this to be a location more suited to their personality—and pocketbook—than a full-blown extravaganza fit for royalty.

~ Consider your college or military chapel or banquet hall. As an alumnus or a veteran, you may have access for a limited charge. For instance, the U.S. Naval Academy in Annapolis, Maryland, is a favorite wedding location for Annapolis graduates and members of the navy and marines, among others.

~ A wedding held at home may be enticing as a free location, but remember to add on the cost of decor and the rental of tables, a chef's tent, and other necessities. Be sure you won't end up paying more than you would for a modest reception hall location.

~ At-home weddings require additional insurance riders, parking permits for large weddings, and usually professional landscaping and cleaning after the big day. Are you sure you want to spend this much money?

~ Perhaps a friend or relative could offer as their wedding gift to you the use of their yacht or nearby vacation home. Those close to you with resources will undoubtedly be honored that you'd even consider their place for your wedding.

Rentals for a Home Wedding

The following is one bride's list of items she had to rent for her at-home wedding. In the end, the cost of the rentals actually added up to more money per guest than if she had held her wedding in a standard banquet hall.

- Large tent for reception
- Bridal arch for ceremony
- Twenty tables for guest seating
- Two long tables for buffet
- Twenty table linens and enough linen napkins for guests
- Chairs (150)
- China place settings (150 sets)
- Crystal and glassware (150 sets)
- Silverware (150 sets)
- Serving platters
- Punch bowl
- Aisle runner
- Portable bar
- Installation of dance floor
- Platform for band
- Booster seats for kids
- And more

A bride who held a smaller wedding inside her home still had to rent china, crystal, glassware, silverware, serving platters, and other items. So be sure to consider the full cost of rentals and the reputation of the rental companies.

> *A close family friend offered the use of his yacht for the wedding, and we respected his property by keeping our guest list small and within control. We planned an intimate wedding for thirty on that boat, and it was lovely.*
>
> —TARA

⌁ By all means, never take advantage of a friend who makes an offer to help you out. To do so is the essence of selfishness, and relationships get mangled and ruined through insensitive behavior. Always be sure to respect a friend's home, property, and feelings. Offer to have his or her home professionally cleaned after the wedding and send a thank-you note or gift.

⌁ Don't take a standby position on a ceremony location waiting list just because it's cheaper. There's too much invested in this wedding for you to depend on a maybe for the most important part of the day.

11

Your Reception Location

You don't have to pay top dollar for a wonderful reception location. Here you'll learn how to save when choosing the best reception hall for your wedding.

~ If you've chosen to have your reception at a reception hall, avoid the top-of-the-line places with the largest ads in the newspaper and the celebrity clientele. Their prices will be inflated by their status as a prime wedding location, and they can sometimes be too gaudy for the average person's tastes. Instead, carefully compare all the choices available to you. Look at the entire package, not just the pretty scenery.

~ Choose a reception location that already has tables, chairs, and equipment so you don't have to rent those separately. Of course, the price for this place may be higher, but you have to consider the value of the items you don't have to rent.

〰 When you're checking out reception halls, consider these points: Is the place clean? How many waiters or servers will be working your reception? How many other receptions will there be at the same time as yours? Are the walls soundproof enough to keep out the sounds of the other receptions? Search out all the details that you think could possibly affect your reception, and question the manager about them. You want to make sure your money is well spent.

〰 Make sure the site has free parking for guests, so that you don't have to pick up the tab for each car parked in a local lot. Some hotels even charge per car, so ask your catering sales associate for a parking charge waiver, if necessary.

〰 Ask about separate site fees. Some botanical gardens where receptions are held charge thousands of dollars just to be on their grounds, on top of reception fees. Don't get blindsided by site charges.

〰 Ask if you will have access to all areas of the grounds, such as gardens and gazebos, for free. Some sites will charge you for taking photos in those areas, and some will surprise you with the news that you *can't* take photos in the garden you originally loved because another wedding has been booked for that area. Don't lose your site dreams because you didn't ask questions and ensure that you have access to the grounds.

~ Comparison shop among reception locations, and keep track of your notes for each so you can check off what each hall offers for its price. Leave space for notes about each place as well. Use their brochure or your printouts of their website pages to keep yourself organized.

~ Make sure your chosen site has insurance so that anything that may go wrong doesn't end up costing *you* a fortune.

~ Consider a smaller, more intimate banquet hall or room for your reception. You may need to trim your guest list slightly, but the price per person is bound to be much lower than for the too-large rooms that drip with crystal and glare with fancy lighting.

~ If your family has a favorite restaurant that you've been going to for years, you obviously already trust its dependability. So don't rule out its reception services just because it's not a new place. That way you don't have to worry whether the food will be good. One bride even received a 33-percent-off credit for her wedding at a favorite restaurant's banquet room just because she and her family had been loyal customers for years.

~ An outdoor setting can add cost for rentals, arrangement of facilities, and more. When you add it all up, make sure you're getting the best deal.

~ If you're planning an outdoor reception, plan an alternate setting in case it rains. To be doubly sure, map out instructions for a quick move in case the skies break with little time to set up in a new place. Having to hold the wedding on a rain date can mean extra expenses and some lost services with no refunds, so it's smart to have a same-day plan B rather than plan a separate rain date for your wedding. The best option is to book a site that has both indoor and outdoor party areas.

~ The arboretum, winery, mansion, or beach setting you arranged for your ceremony will work just as beautifully for your reception. Besides, having a setting work double duty for you means you won't have to worry about transportation from the ceremony to the reception. That could mean a total of five hundred dollars or more in your pocket. See how savings just pile up when you're looking for them?

↝ One last reception setting option: you can transform a social association's multipurpose party room or a church hall into a pretty locale for your celebration. It may take some extra yards of material, a creative team, and some work, but it can be done nicely. Some organizations even can spruce up the place for you for a small donation to their cause.

Renting Reception Items

The reception location you choose may require you to rent such items as tables, chairs, china, chafing dishes, and linens. Save money in this arena with the following tips.

↝ Know exactly what you need to rent for the reception hall. Get table, floor, and bandstand sizes and have the correct layout and measurements of the room where your wedding will be held. Most reception halls will provide preprinted layouts with dimensions for this use. Always see the items you'll be renting to be sure they're in good condition and to ensure a table for twelve will sit twelve comfortably. Remember that your guests will use more than one plate and glass each. Figure three plates for buffet use, one plate for each course, and several drinking glasses throughout the night. Always order more than you think you'll need, as it would be a major gaffe to run out of clean glasses during your reception. Planning for rental items is a great way to save not just money but the reception's success.

~ Look at the items you're arranging to rent before you commit to them. The china may be hideous and the glasses chipped.

~ Carefully review all items when they are delivered, noting broken or marred pieces to prevent your having to pay damages. Have the delivery person record the damages and sign this record. Several months ago, a bride didn't get this proof, and the company made her replace twenty chipped wine goblets.

~ Have the items cleaned afterward, if those are the terms of your contract, and ready to be returned on time. A delay may mean extra charges. Similarly, know if you *don't* have to clean them. Some companies say "just rinse and return to the rack," so be aware of the requirements so that your unneeded cleaning efforts don't make you late in returning the items.

~ Simply use your own china and glassware if you have enough of a similar style to go around, or borrow from friends and relatives. Items such as punch bowls and candelabras don't need to be rented. You can use your own.

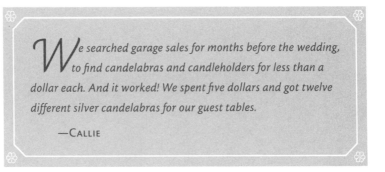

We searched garage sales for months before the wedding, to find candelabras and candleholders for less than a dollar each. And it worked! We spent five dollars and got twelve different silver candelabras for our guest tables.

—CALLIE

∽ Be sure your rental company is affiliated with the American Rental Association (ararental.org). You always want to hire a professional.

∽ Be sure delivery is free. If not, ask the groomsmen or family friends to pick up or drop off your rental order.

12

Religious, Spiritual, and Cultural Elements of the Ceremony

The officiant comes with a price tag. Booking the church or synagogue may mean extra expenses. Find out how to save on ceremony fees.

The Ceremony Officiant

~ Comparison shop for officiant fees. Some charge as little as one hundred dollars, and some actually ask for six hundred to seven hundred dollars. You can save a lot by knowing that there are some pricing options when shopping for a qualified officiant.

~ To find an officiant near you, visit celebrantsusa.com.

∽ Ask your wedding experts and recently married friends for referrals to their own favorite officiants. Word of mouth will always get you the best candidates with appropriate pricing.

∽ Never hire an officiant based only on an online ad. Always meet in person with the officiant to gauge his or her personality and personal preferences for running ceremonies. Some less-than-official officiants are out there, and you don't want your wedding ruined by strange readings and theatrics by a loony officiant.

∽ Keep in mind that you will often have to pay an officiant's travel expenses. So try to choose a local expert over a long-distance one.

∽ If your wedding will be interfaith, you might require the ceremony leadership of an officiant team—a minister and a rabbi, for instance. This will often mean two separate payments for these officiants, so ask about their individual fees so that your budget doesn't get ruined by a double-fee surprise.

∽ An interesting new development on the officiant scene is that some websites will ordain people for the day through an uncomplicated application system and a short waiting period. Ordination certificates are also available through the Internet for any interested individuals, *but you have to make sure these are legal in your state* (ask your town marriage license registrar). If you'd love a family member to perform the service, perhaps he or she can become ordained for the day. Check this carefully, as you need to be sure the credentials are valid.

Religious Elements

∼ Ask your officiant for a copy of the guidelines and restrictions of your church or synagogue. Ask questions to clarify. Certain things may not be allowed in your ceremony—such as a unity candle or a secular song performed by a professional singer—and it's best to find out before you spend money on them.

∼ If you need to do some research on the religious elements of your ceremony or reception, research customs of your faith online, in books from the library, and through your officiant. No need to pay money for a "religious advisor's fee."

∼ If you need special ceremonial items, such as a satin ring bearer's pillow, a white aisle runner, or a chuppah, make or borrow them if you can. Or see if your church or synagogue has one you can borrow. Mandy regrets not having done this.

Her florist charged her $125 for an aisle runner that looked like a giant paper towel roll.

～ Don't plan to add on to any religious ritual or practice unless you've talked to the officiant about it. Most officiants have their own rules, and these must not be altered without permission. Also, ask if photography and videography are allowed. Some sites forbid intrusive flashes and spotlights.

～ If you wish to include readings and a performance of music in your religious ceremony, a relative or friend can read a religious passage, play an instrument, or sing a hymn as a gift to you, rather than your hiring experts.

～ Ask if you can arrange for the church choir or soloist to perform at your ceremony for a lower price than professional musicians might charge, or for free! Some chorales and children's choirs will perform for no charge, valuing the public performance as practice for their upcoming competitions and big holiday shows.

～ Your church or synagogue office may have a list of approved musicians you can interview and audition for performance on your day. It is important to make sure the site doesn't prohibit you from hiring anyone other than their sanctioned pros. You'll have to cancel your booking and lose your deposit money.

~ If proof of annulment or divorce is needed, don't pay extra fees for the church to locate copies of your legal paperwork. You can send for copies yourself or get free notarized copies of your own documents.

~ Some churches require marrying couples to attend premarital classes. If yours is one that does, comparison shop among classes and ask your church if it will accept a certificate of completion from a course taken at another church. Some churches, unfortunately, demand that you take their course at their fee. Take that into consideration when looking for a place to hold your ceremony.

Spiritual Elements

~ Research spiritual traditions online for free, including readings, vows, symbols, and rites, so that you don't have to hire a coordinator or book the "research package" of your spiritual officiant for extra money.

∽ Provide your own food and drink, such as a loaf of bread or bottle of wine, for use in spiritual rituals, rather than arranging for the site or caterer to get them. The professionals may charge you ten dollars for that loaf of bread and thirty dollars for that bottle of wine. You can purchase your own for far less.

∽ If you'll incorporate handfasting in your spiritual ceremony, don't overspend on braided cord from a spiritual wedding supply company. Go to the craft store to buy a yard of braided cord for less than five dollars.

∽ Use piped-in spiritual music, such as Native American flute music, for your ceremony, rather than tracking down professional musicians and hiring them to play at your ceremony. Your site may have a great sound system for the perfect musical accompaniment (for free!), and you can use your own CDs or MP3s.

∽ Looking for a live musician? Ask around at a yoga studio or spiritual wellness studio for referrals, often for far less than expert musicians who play weddings for a living. These non-wedding musicians often charge half the fee of expert acts.

Cultural Elements

∼ Check online to find a cultural association or club that can guide you toward specialty cultural musicians, item rentals or budget-priced purchases, and other discounts made possible by virtue of this group *not* being affiliated with the wedding industry. Many cultural associations work to keep their traditions alive, so they'll be happy to assist you and support your cultural wedding elements.

∼ Ask if the cultural association offers catering, which may be a "club" of group members who prepare specialty cultural food items for far less than a caterer's fees . . . and the food is often far more authentic and delicious! Just make sure the group is licensed and insured and has been inspected for food safety. All food service professionals must have these official documents to be sure the meal you eat is safe.

∼ Ask if the cultural association can recommend musicians specializing in cultural music, plus professional dancers and performers as participants in the ceremony. Again, these groups list entertainers for budget prices and are a great resource.

~ Ask friends and family if you can borrow their own cultural wedding props, as a way to add more personalization to your day and save you money.

~ Research online to learn how to make a crown or wreath of olive leaves, or any other greenery or floral pieces needed for cultural traditions. With good do-it-yourself instructions, you'll often only need to invest a few dollars in greenery, rather than pay an expert forty to fifty dollars to make the wreaths for you.

~ Check out *Wedding Dresses* magazine (weddingdresses .com), which lists lots of cultural wedding ideas and resources.

13

Your Gown

The average bride spends between one thousand and three thousand dollars on her gown. I've even heard of some blank-check brides throwing down a whopping one hundred thousand dollars for a dress that's to be worn only once. The wedding gown industry is filled with over-the-top designs and prices to match, but there are plenty of low-cost options that will make you look just as beautiful on your wedding day. Don't think those outrageous price tags are all that's out there. There are ways to get a beautiful gown for less.

Where to Look

∼ Start looking right away. Give yourself plenty of time to search out the perfect gown. Most brides who rushed spent hundreds of dollars more on their gowns. The average number of gowns that brides try on is six.

∼ Don't order the gown before you have a date set for the wedding. If you order a summer gown and it turns out your wedding will have to be held in the winter, you'll lose money when you have to cancel your gown and order another.

∼ Be careful at the big, fancy bridal gown salons. You may think they're a great source of everything you need, and to some brides they may be, but you might not get the best prices there. Salons are expensive (how else do you think they pay

Average Spending for Attire and Hair/Makeup

	2008	2009	2010	2011	2012	2013
Bride accessories	$319	$324	$329	$334	$339	$345
Groom accessories	$197	$200	$203	$206	$209	$212
Groom suit/tux	$252	$256	$260	$264	$268	$272
Hair/makeup service	$166	$171	$176	$181	$187	$193
Headpiece/veil	$318	$323	$328	$333	$339	$345
Wedding dress	$1,266	$1,287	$1,308	$1,330	$1,352	$1,374

Printed with permission from TheWeddingReport.com.

for all those lights, the plush pink carpeting, and the free cappuccino?), and an aggressive salesperson may pressure you into spending more money than you'd planned. After all, if she works on commission, she gets a bigger cut of whatever you wind up paying. On top of the gown, you may also pay high prices for alterations. Include these salons in your research, but don't limit yourself to them.

⌒ Ask friends to refer you to the great bridal shop or formal dress shop where they got their gorgeous wedding gowns for less. You'll enjoy the fruits of their research and bargain hunting.

⌒ Get on the mailing lists at several bridal and dress shops, so that you're alerted—sometimes with VIP status before public announcements—of in-store sales and designer trunk sales where you can find gowns at 60 percent off, if not more. Most shops hold clearance sales to make room for the new lines of dresses coming in, so they'd rather sell their stock to you for less than take a financial loss.

⌒ Don't miss designer trunk shows and sample sales where designer gowns can be found at markdowns as low as 60 to 70 percent off. You'll find advertisements for these wonderful sales in bridal magazines, on bridal websites, and in the newspaper's special bridal inserts. Some bridal salons even host trunk shows of their own, so call and ask for schedules and appointments.

∽ Ask the shop clerk about any gowns that are being discontinued and therefore offered at a special discount price. One bride found her dream gown this way. She learned it was on the discontinued list, ordered one of the remaining ones in the company's stock, and saved two hundred dollars.

∽ Ask about sample sales, where dress shops put their floor model dresses on sale for 50 to 75 percent off. Yes, dozens of brides have tried these on, and they may have scuff marks at the bottom of the hem, but the seamstress can often clean any marks. Shorter brides say hem marks are cut off to shorten the dress! It's a steal!

∽ Look through bridal magazines and catalogs to get an idea of what you really like. If you've purchased the magazine or received it as a gift, tear out the pages of the gowns you like and keep them together as possibilities. Just remember: the gowns pictured on those pages or on websites are not exactly the designer's least expensive options. So don't fall in love with a picture. Be open to finding a less expensive gown of that same style, using the shape of a skirt or the design of a bodice as inspiration for a less expensive gown.

∽ Check bridal gown designers' websites for their special lines of more moderately priced dresses. Many designers have established these more affordable collections to capture a wider audience of shoppers (brides who can't spent fifty thousand dollars on a dress!).

~ So where should you look if not in the big bridal salons? Start in smaller bridal salons. You'll find them online or in ads in your local bridal magazines. They need to make less profit on each gown because they don't have to worry about upkeep on their marble floors and chandeliers. Of course, by opting away from the big salon you're sacrificing the posh, first-class service, but if you're determined to save money on nonessentials you'll find the smaller stores offer just as much of what you really need.

I had one gown in mind—and I didn't want any gown but that one. I checked in the big stores and in the catalogs, but no go. I guess it was too simple and classic a style for them to keep in stock. And then one day on a whim I walked into a quaint little bridal store that was no bigger than my kitchen, and there it was! The one gown I wanted, just hanging there like it was waiting for me. The woman behind the counter was so nice, she even suggested an outstanding seamstress whose prices were the lowest in the area. I was so pleased, I ordered my bridesmaids' gowns from there, too.

*—*SHEA

Bridal Gown Designers

To save you some time and keep you organized, here are the websites of some of the biggest gown designers. Asterisks indicate the designers who offer selections of beautiful gowns and dresses for less than the standard one thousand to three thousand dollars that most brides pay. Keep in mind that more designers are sure to have established "budget collections" since the time of this writing, so check each website out thoroughly and don't be afraid to call the 800 number listed on the site to ask about discontinued or sale dresses. Look also for their list of "trunk sales" where gowns are sold at steep discounts—even the top name designers need to unload last season's gowns!

Alfred Angelo—alfredangelo.com

*America's Bridal Discounters—bridaldiscounters.com

*Amsale—amsale.com

Birnbaum and Bullock—birnbaumandbullock.com

Bonny—bonny.com

Bridal Originals—bridaloriginals.com

Carolina Herrera—carolinaherrera.com

Christos, Inc.—christos.com

David's Bridal—davidsbridal.com

Demetrios—demetrios.com

Diamond Collection—diamondcollection.com

*Eden Bridals—edenbridals.com

Emme Bridal—emmebridal.com

Forever Yours—foreverbridals.com

*Jasmine Collection—jasminebridal.com

*Jessica McClintock—jessicamcclintock.com

Jim Hjelm—jimhjelmvisions.com

*Lili—lilibridals.com

Manale—manalecom

*Melissa Sweet Bridal Collection—melissasweet.com

Michelle Roth—michelleroth.com

Mon Cheri—mcbridals.com

Mori Lee—morilee.com

Priscilla of Boston—priscillaofboston.com

Private Label by G—privatelabelbyg.com

*Sweetheart—gowns.com

Tomasina—tomasinabridal.com

*Venus—venusbridal.com

Vera Wang—verawang.com

Yumi Katsura—yumikatsura.com

An asterisk (*) indicates companies with lower-priced gown options.

⤳ If you're able to, look at bridal stores in different parts of your city, different cities, or even different states. In a "richer" area, you're likely to find that prices are higher because the clientele can afford the amount asked. In more middle-class areas, prices are a bit lower. You may be able to find your dream dress across town for a hundred dollars less. Or your cousin in Delaware may find the dress for much less than its New York price tag.

⤳ When you're searching for a gown in several bridal shops, comparison shop like crazy. Take note of each store's policy on alterations, ordering time, refund rules, and flexibility. Check the quality of their work. Is the on-site seamstress frazzled and looking way behind schedule? Is the stock in good condition and relatively new? What kinds of guarantees can they give you? It pays to put in the time to compare the places that might outfit you on your wedding day. You'll want the best quality service your budget can buy. One bride used a notebook to record facts, figures, and observations about each bridal shop she considered. Her research paid off well—the shop she chose ended up saving her two hundred dollars more than the others would have.

⤳ Look at dress shops and their websites, such as Ann Taylor (anntaylor.com), where their Celebrations dress line often offers on-sale formal dresses.

〜 Look on eBay for designer gowns at a fraction of retail costs. Not only are recent brides selling their once-worn gowns, but bridal shop owners regularly "unload" their stock to make room for incoming collections. You could save 70 percent. Just shop wisely whenever you're buying online.

〜 Check consignment shops nearby and in ritzier neighborhoods for gowns that are up for sale by women who want to make a percentage of their money back. You'll find thousand-dollar gowns on sale for a third of their original price, if not less.

〜 If you have a friend or relative who works in a dress shop or a department store, see if she'll let you use her employee's discount. A savings of 10 to 20 percent off a five-hundred-dollar gown is fifty to a hundred dollars.

〜 Look in the formals sections of major department stores. While business there may have been crowded out in the past by fancy salons, brides today are coming back to the basics in gown shopping. They're looking for quality and a good price again, so the glitz of a salon may not be their first choice anymore. After the winter holidays and at the end of summer, a wide range of formal gowns are on sale. You may be able to shop now for next season's wedding for 50 percent off!

⁓ In a bridal shop or department store, look on the brides-maid dress rack for pretty white, off-white, or pastel gowns that may work perfectly as your wedding dress. These are often priced at less than $150, so there's your great find!

⁓ Ask the manager when the new shipment of gowns is scheduled to arrive. With advance notice, you might be able to beat the crowds for the nicest but most inexpensive in the bunch.

Check with the Better Business Bureau

When narrowing down choices, check with your state's Better Business Bureau to see if the companies are clear. Have there been any complaints or reports against them? At worst, are they operating illegally? We've all heard the horror stories about the dress shops that mysteriously disappeared in the middle of the night, leaving hundreds of brides without their gowns and the thousands of dollars they paid for them the week before the wedding. Unfortunately, it has happened, and it could happen again. So consult the reporting agency to see if your store is legitimate and free of suspicious record. When you're dealing with something as important as your gown, it's best to protect yourself from all angles.

More Wedding Gown Sources

~ Take a photo to a quality seamstress for her to make a copy of a designer gown, at a fraction of the price.

~ Buy a friend's wedding gown from her! If she doesn't want to preserve it and you love the style, you can buy it for a low price and then take it to a seamstress for fixing up.

~ Look into wedding gown rentals. Many shops now offer this service. They go to designer trunk sales, buy gorgeous gowns, and rent them no more than three times for just a hundred or two hundred dollars per wearing. This is a great way to get that Vera Wang!

~ Brides-to-be have found beautiful gowns for as little as forty or fifty dollars at the outlets. Look online at outlet bound.com to find outlet stores, and head out for a day of sure-thing cut prices up to 60, 70, even 80 percent off.

~ Believe it or not, some of the most beautiful ivory and off-white gowns can be found at antique shops. Krissy found a 1930 antique hand-beaded wedding dress for less than two hundred dollars. Scout the shops in the center of town, ask for help (most antique-store owners are aware of what's in stock in other antique stores), and even browse through some of the antique shows you've seen advertised in the paper.

Choosing the Best Gown

◆ Be sure the gown you choose fits the level of formality of your wedding. You won't wear an ultraformal gown with a ten-foot train to a tea party in the garden. Staying within your level of formality will keep you from spending too much on a too-fancy gown.

Check Quality

Make sure the gown is of good quality. Inspect the seams and stitches to ensure that it's been made well. You don't want your investment to fall apart on you.

◆ Buy a simple gown. Beads and bangles often raise the price of the gown and the care it requires. If you like the beaded look, you can always add your own or have a friend do the work for you. Tammy bought a simple gown for two hundred dollars and bought fifty dollars worth of pearls and beads to stitch onto her neckline and bodice. When she was finished, her wedding gown looked identical to an eight-hundred-dollar store-bought wedding gown.

∾ Buy a gown in a less expensive material. Do your home-work on fabric prices. Compare satin, taffeta, silk, crisp cotton, and so on at fabric.com. For instance, silk shantung is more expensive than silk chiffon and silk organza, French satin is slightly less expensive than those, and plain chiffon is lower priced than all. Your designer contends with market price on all materials, but it helps if you know which fabrics are the priciest to make an informed decision.

∾ Gowns in color may be priced lower than traditional bridal white, so ask if the gown you love comes in a pale blush color for less. It's a trend for brides to wear color, so see if this works for you.

∾ A shorter tea-length or suit dress is often going to be less expensive than a full-length gown with a ten-foot train. Just make sure it fits the formality of your wedding.

Shopping Smart

~ If you find that a full-priced gown on a dress shop rack has a tiny, fixable flaw, ask the store manager if you can have that gown for a discount. After all, other brides might not take it in its current condition. A flawed gown can almost always be mended. So don't walk past that "irregular" rack, either. Maya found a pretty off-white gown that had a torn side seam. A simple repair would do the trick, she knew, but the store considered it damaged goods and knocked seventy-five dollars off the price just to get it off their rack.

~ Shop early in the day. You have more energy for comparison shopping, and you're more likely to be focused on the one job at hand.

~ When shopping, the input of others can influence you to choose a more expensive gown. If everyone is cooing, "Oh, you look fabulous in that other one," you may be swayed by group opinion to choose a more expensive gown than the one you love equally. The best shopping strategy is to go by yourself or with one other person for an objective opinion.

~ When choosing your gown, no matter where you're shopping, always consider your body type and whether that dress is right for you. Does it make you look shorter? Is it accentuating your hips? Is it too tight? Is it too low cut? You don't want to buy a dress that doesn't make you look your best.

~ Don't trust a sale sign without checking to see if the price is really better. The thousand-dollar price tag you see marked out in red pen and then replaced with a $750 tag may just be a ploy to make you think you're getting a huge discount. This is where comparison shopping is crucial.

~ Order your correct dress size according to the manufacturer's measurements so you won't have to pay for major alterations. Some dress shops order larger sizes intentionally so the buyer has to pay to have the dress taken in. Similarly, don't order a dress size smaller than what you are right now because you're planning to lose thirty pounds by your wedding day. At worst, you won't lose all the weight and you'll be stuck with a too-small gown that doesn't look good on you. Instead, order your current size and don't worry about the cost of alterations.

~ Order a wedding gown that can be cut to a shorter length, trimmed of embellishments, and worn again. It's good money sense to spend that much for a dress you will be able to wear again.

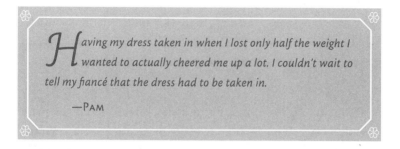

Having my dress taken in when I lost only half the weight I wanted to actually cheered me up a lot. I couldn't wait to tell my fiancé that the dress had to be taken in.

—PAM

〜 When paying for your gown, use a credit card. You'll have an easier time getting reimbursed if something should go wrong.

〜 Keep all sales slips as a record of the date you ordered the dress, the specifics of the dress, and its size, and as an added precaution, get the salesperson to sign it as a record of who sold the dress to you. Trouble can be cleared up easily with that information. In addition, have the seamstress write down your measurements and the store-recommended dress size on the order form. If a gown is ordered that's too small and a reorder is necessary, you'll have the proof for them to pay expenses.

〜 Keep a record of the promised date of delivery, too, so you can get on the phone if your dress is late.

∼ During fittings, ensure the correct fit by wearing the bra, slip, and shoes you'll be wearing on your wedding day. They can affect the way the dress hangs on you, and wearing them at every fitting will save you money on last-minute alterations. One bride unfortunately had to pay fifty dollars in last-minute alteration fees at her final fitting because her selection of wedding underwear made the dress a little too snug. Yet another bride found that her new corset-style strapless bra was just enough to keep the back zipper on her gown from closing all the way, so she had to do without it.

∼ Try to buy your gown at a shop that offers free alterations using their team of on-site experts. This perk can add up to two hundred dollars saved. Of course, the dresses have to be well priced for this to be worth it, but it's important to keep in mind.

∼ If alterations come at a fee, do some research to see if you can find a better-priced professional alterations expert, and bring your dress to that person instead. Ask recently married friends for suggestions, and other wedding experts can recommend candidates as well (your florist knows everyone in the business!). You may be able to save hundreds of dollars just by taking your dress down the street to an independent, seasoned seamstress.

14

Your Shoes and Accessories

Two hundred dollars for a pair of simple white shoes? I'm amazed at what some brides will spend to have the best of everything on their wedding day. Your shoes and accessories are just a small part of your wedding look, accents to your radiant beauty. Read on to learn how to get great shoes and accessories without spending a fortune.

Your Shoes

∼ Don't order shoes in a bridal salon. The price will be much higher than in a regular shoe store. One price test turned up a fifty-dollar difference in identical shoes sold at a regular store versus a bridal salon.

～ Don't order "bridal shoes" as marketed on websites and in stores. Just by adding the word "bridal" or "wedding," the marketers tend to charge more for them. Buy regular pretty shoes instead.

～ Collect coupons for your favorite shoe store and use those, as well as any sale discounts, to buy your wedding shoes. The end of summer is often a great time to buy wedding-appropriate shoes on sale!

～ Visit outletbound.com to find terrific shoe outlets for discount heels.

～ Visit eBay to find designer shoes at deep discounts, often two-hundred-dollar shoes available for thirty or so dollars!

～ Take advantage of post-prom season sales in May and June to buy pretty strappy heels in white, silver, or color for up to 50 percent off! They're making room for their fall collections, so everything must go . . . for a bargain.

～ For a great price cut, order the same style shoes your bridesmaids will be wearing so you're a part of their group order discount. Yours may even be free with a group order of, say, four pairs or more. Just be sure your pair isn't sent to be dyed with theirs. Visit dyeables.com to see if their styles and prices work well for you.

> **Compare and Save**
> Beaded, appliquéd "bridal" shoes $200
> Plain two-inch-heel shoes ....$30–$40

∼ Visit a discount shoe store, like Payless or MJM, and shop there. Inspect your choices for quality as well as price. A fifteen-dollar pair of shoes is no bargain if they fall apart after two uses.

∼ Visit ninashoes.com for a great line of wedding-appropriate shoes at low prices.

∼ Look for seasonal in-store shoe sales. A 50-percent-off clearance will take the bite out of shoe prices. Ask your friends to let you know about shoe sales they see near them. You could visit them and go shoe shopping together!

∼ Keep an eye out for the Victoria's Secret shoe catalog and shoe sales online. You may be able to find a stylish silver shoe that works perfectly with your gown.

∼ Wear ballerina slippers. They're light and comfortable, they look charming and romantic, and they're inexpensive as well, often as low as ten dollars a pair.

∼ Shop for your shoes later in the afternoon when your feet are naturally swollen. Shoes that fit in the morning may be tight on you during your evening reception, so think ahead and use this general rule of shoe shopping so that you don't have to buy another pair.

∼ For the ultimate in savings, wear a pair of white or silver dress shoes you already own. Just make sure they look nice, not old, scraped, and worn in the heel. You may be lifting up your dress to reveal your garter later on in the reception, and you won't want to reveal your savings in the shoe department at the same time. This only works if shoes you already own are suitable for the formality of your wedding. Many brides have used this idea and have reported that they loved being in comfortable, broken-in shoes they knew would fit.

Your Veil

The veil you'll wear depends on the formality of your wedding and your dress. Be sure of the basics before you shop, to avoid having to return your choice for a loss of money.

~ Comparison shop for veils in bridal salons' sale racks. Veils get discontinued, too, so you will often find these at 20 to 50 percent off.

~ Bridal shops do sell their floor model veils for discounted prices as well, so ask about that. Veils rarely get marked or torn in the store.

~ Wear your mother's wedding veil. It will mean a lot to both of you, and you'll probably only have to pay for a cleaning and alteration to your height. Or borrow a relative's veil if she seems receptive to the idea. Siblings, grandmothers, godmothers, great-grandparents—all are likely to bestow the honor.

~ Designer trunk sales also include veils, so visit several shows even if you don't need a gown.

~ Try eBay as a great source for buying veils, since size isn't as big an issue as it is with dresses, and you could find a beautiful designer veil for twenty or thirty dollars instead of two hundred.

~ Consignment shops are also great sources for veils at discount prices, up to 50 percent off.

∾ Share a veil purchase with a friend or relative who is marrying around the same time as you. If you can both agree on a style and length you love, that's 50 percent off the price when you split the bill.

∾ Buy a plain veil and add your own crystal embellishments using crystals from the craft store. You might even choose to sew on a delicate appliqué to the end of the veil, an effect that often costs a lot in designer veils.

∾ Have a talented relative or friend make your veil for you, perhaps using a fabric headband, netting, and some pearls. Tear out a picture of the kind of veil you'd like, and let the artist make this her wedding gift to you. Or make your own veil if you have the time and the talent. One bride's aunt made the bride's veil from some tulle, a fabric headband, and some pearls. Her gorgeous creation cost just thirty dollars to make and was even prettier than the two-hundred-dollar styles that you find in the stores.

∾ You can find easy-to-use make-your-own-veil kits at most major craft stores for less than thirty dollars. These come with standard hair combs and headbands, material, and accessories, plus simple instructions for a talented crafter to use.

⌁ Decide if you would like to skip the veil. For informal or nonreligious weddings, it may be appropriate for you to go without one.

Your Headpiece

⌁ Bridal salon tiaras are expensive, costing several hundred dollars. You can get a beautiful tiara from a bridal salon when you attend a trunk sale. Accessories like these are often included in the sales.

⌁ Visit an accessories shop at the mall to find pretty tiaras close to prom time: March through May. Inspect them closely to make sure they're attractive and well made. Some tiaras at accessories shops are considered toys, so watch out for shoddy gemstone applications.

⌁ Borrow a recently married friend's or relative's wedding tiara for your own wedding as a freebie!

⌁ Check eBay for pretty tiaras. Shop owners, recently married brides, and crafters who *make* tiaras sell their tiaras there for discounts of 30 to 50 percent off what they'd cost in a bridal shop.

∽ An arrangement of baby rosebuds and baby's breath can be tucked into a hair clip that holds up a French twist. There's no need to order this to be made at extra cost by your florist; just experiment ahead of time and do it yourself.

∽ Don't buy a jeweled hair clip at a department store for a hundred dollars. Go to a craft store where they have simple silver hair clips for less than twenty dollars. Or borrow another bride's jeweled hair clip for your big day. Your sister may be willing to lend you hers as your "something borrowed." Brides don't think to ask others for these accessories, and it's a great way to find a hidden freebie!

∽ You'll find pearl- or crystal-studded hairpins at the craft store for less than five dollars per pack of six. Your hairstylist can push these into a pretty updo for a celebrity look at a bargain.

∽ Look in the craft store for a pretty satin-covered headband for less than ten dollars. They offer these to be embellished, but you may find the simple look is best.

∽ Or choose instead not to wear any headpiece at all. Just make sure this option conforms to your wedding location's rules and the degree of formality of the wedding. Skip the veil and headpiece and just let your hair be the focal point of your look. Talented hairstylists can create veritable sculptures from your hair using upsweeps, twists, braids, and tendrils. Accentuate your 'do with inexpensive pearl or jeweled hairpins or tiny fresh flowers, and you've only spent thirty to forty dollars.

Your Lingerie

~ Don't buy a corset at the bridal shop. Visit department stores, especially at sale time, to get a great selection for less.

~ Watch the Victoria's Secret sales for discounts on corsets, strapless bras, and other undergarments.

~ Visit a lingerie shop to try on corsets, and then look online to find the same model number. I found my wedding day corset for 40 percent off by shopping this way.

~ Your wedding night lingerie can be a gift from your groom, instead of pricier jewelry.

~ There's no need for you to buy a crinoline. Most gowns come with a crinoline already in the skirt.

〜 Use your bridal shower gift cards for lingerie shops to buy your wedding day undergarments.

〜 Since you'll undoubtedly want to keep your garter as a precious memento of your wedding day, you should have two garters: one to keep and one to throw. Buy what brides call a "cheapie" in a lingerie store for the tossing. Note: the garter toss is becoming passé. You may choose to skip this outdated custom entirely.

〜 Check party supply stores and card stores for inexpensive garter sets for less than twenty dollars.

〜 Buy basic stockings. While designer-name fancy silk kinds with patterns or the little design at the ankle are great indulgences for the bride, they're also a place where money can be saved without noticeable loss. You'll feel just as wonderful on your wedding day whether or not your stockings cost forty dollars.

〜 Look for designer stocking such as those from Wolford on eBay for 40 percent less.

〜 Take advantage of winter holiday mega-sales at Victoria's Secret to buy your wedding day stockings for 60 percent off.

~ Visit alexblake.com to find great-priced designer bridal stockings.

~ Have an extra pair of stockings in your emergency bag (more on this later) in case of a noticeable run. If you have splurged on expensive silk stockings for your originals, the extra pair definitely should be the more generic of the two you've purchased.

~ Look for gloves at bridal shop trunk sales. They often sell the formal elbow-length gloves for 60 to 70 percent off at these events. Formal gloves can also be found for less than ten dollars on eBay.

~ Skip all the extras, like gloves and parasols. They're the essence of nonessential. One bride's total for gloves, a parasol, and jeweled hair clips for under her veil was $180. That amount could be better used elsewhere—like the honeymoon.

Your Jewelry

~ Don't buy new jewelry for your wedding. It's very likely that your groom's wedding gift to you will be fine jewelry of some sort, and you'll want to wear that.

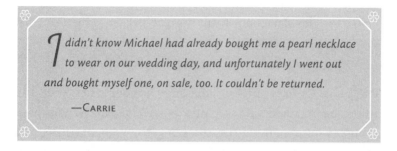

I didn't know Michael had already bought me a pearl necklace to wear on our wedding day, and unfortunately I went out and bought myself one, on sale, too. It couldn't be returned.

—CARRIE

~ Jewelry, if not a gift, also makes a wonderful "something borrowed" choice. Wear an heirloom necklace or earrings, perhaps the pearls your mother wore at her wedding.

~ If your gown bodice is detailed, or if you'll wear dramatic dangle earrings, you may wish to skip the pricey diamond necklace, which isn't needed when you have so much else going on visually.

~ Wear your own sparkly jewelry instead of getting something new. It adds to the history of pieces you've received from your parents or your groom. As one bride says, "Sparkle is sparkle."

~ Think a year ahead when it comes to all of your accessories and shop now when you see big holiday sales pop up. These items won't go out of style, and size doesn't matter.

15

Dressing the Bridal Party

Your attendants are honored to be chosen as part of your bridal party, but you don't want to sour the mood by burdening them with too high a financial commitment for their wedding day attire. Here you'll find out how to make the right selections to save them money.

Bridesmaids and Junior Bridesmaids

Gowns

∼ While some brides like to purchase their bridesmaids' gowns as gifts for them, you'd do well to allow them to buy their own dresses. Most expect that they'll have to anyway.

Bridesmaids' and Mothers' Gowns

After Six—aftersix.com

Alfred Angelo—alfredangelo.com

Ann Taylor—anntaylor.com

*Bill Levkoff—billlevkoff.com

Chadwick's of Boston Special Occasions—chadwicksof
boston.com

Champagne Formals—champagneformals.com

David's Bridal—davidsbridal.com

Dessy Creations—dessy.com

Galina—galina.com

J Crew—jcrew.com

*JCPenney—jcpenney.com

*Jessica McClintock—jessicamcclintock.com

Lord & Taylor—lordandtaylor.com

Lazaro—lazaro.com

*Macy's—macys.com

*Melissa Sweet Bridal Collection—melissasweet.com

Mon Cheri—moncheribridals.com

Silhouettes—silhouettesmaids.com

Spiegel—spiegel.com

Vera Wang—verawang.com

Watters and Watters—watters.com

An asterisk (*) indicates companies with lower-priced gown options.

~ Get referrals from friends and family members to the bridesmaid dress shops they loved where prices were attractive. Word of mouth is the best way to find steals and great customer service.

~ Sign yourself up on mailing lists to be alerted to bridesmaid dress trunk sales so that you can bring your bridesmaids to these bargain events.

~ Ask at the bridal shop about discontinued dress styles that your maids can still order from the manufacturer. Sometimes the makers haven't stopped creating them, they're just on the way out.

Shop with Your Bridesmaids

Go with your maids to the dress shop so that you'll all have a say in the dresses they'll be wearing. You'll want them to choose a dress to match the formality of your wedding and to complement your gown, and they'll want to make sure an unflattering style and color are not chosen for them. One bride, for instance, chose a dress for all four of her attendants. The two women with larger-than-average chests looked even larger, and the other two looked like sticks. No one was happy, especially at $130 a dress.

⌒ Let the maids choose their own styles of gowns in their price ranges in the same color, ideally from the same store. Everyone will coordinate well, and you eliminate the hassles of who can't afford the gown that the other maids love and whose derriere is too big for that style. Everyone gets a gown that fits her well, compliments her shape, fits her budget, and suits the formality of the occasion.

⌒ Look online at davidsbridal.com to allow your bridesmaids to choose different styles of tops and skirts in the same collection, sometimes on sale for a big percentage off.

⌒ If you have only two or three bridesmaids, you should look for dresses in department stores. A store is more likely to have enough gowns on the rack in your maids' sizes. That wouldn't be the case with eight maids, more than likely, so you've saved again by choosing a smaller bridal party.

⌒ Always hunt for group discounts when you're looking for bridesmaids' dresses. Ask even if one isn't offered. Marisa made the question of group discounts a part of her search and comparison of stores. When she found a company that offered group discounts, each of her attendants saved 20 percent on her dress.

〜 Another reason to look in department stores for your maids' gowns is that prices there are likely to be much lower than those in the bridal shops, especially with coupons and storewide sales. Also look in smaller dress shops for better prices and perhaps better service.

〜 Prom and party dresses are very often ordered as bridesmaids' gowns. Just be sure to shop outside of prom season because prices may be elevated due to demand. The best time to shop may be pre–pre-prom season and post-prom season when dressy dresses are overstocked and up for clearance. Pretty bridesmaids' dresses can be found on the post-prom rack for as low as $30, marked down from $120.

〜 Encourage your bridesmaids to shop from the sale collections at anntaylor.com and other clothing sites and stores with formal dress lines.

〜 Shop at outlets, found through outletbound.com. Your bridesmaids can find their dresses for 50 to 60 percent off.

〜 Ask your bridesmaids if they already have pretty black cocktail dresses that they can wear for your wedding. Have them all show you the dresses first, and this may be a wonderful way to prevent spending anything on their dresses!

~ Encourage your maids to choose a style of dress they'll be able to wear again to formal dinners, dances, and the like. A hundred-dollar dress is a better deal when it's used ten times.

~ Shop at bridal shops that offer free alterations. If the bridal shop charges for its alteration package, you might choose to pass. Hint: do not depend on a friend for this. Go professional; a shoddy sewing job is a glaring example of trying too hard to save.

~ Find a good seamstress or tailor to hire for much less than the dress shop's rates. Get references and comparison shop. Savings here can be anywhere from fifty to a hundred dollars.

Order Gowns Together

If your bridesmaids all live in different cities, have them send you their professionally taken measurements on size cards and checks for their dresses. Then you take those size cards to the dress shop you've chosen so that you can order your maids' gowns for them. Do not allow your maids to order their gowns in shops near their homes because batches of gowns may differ in hue according to which factory they were made in. Always order the gowns in one place; then send them to your maids.

〜 Send the gowns via priority mail, and insure them and request delivery confirmation when you mail them to your maids. This is no time for a dress to get lost in the mail, nor to buy a replacement dress. Federal Express or UPS may be an extra expense, but it's well worth it because missing shipments can be tracked.

〜 As an alternative to this setup, assign your maid or matron of honor the task of ordering and delivering gowns, especially if she lives close to the bridesmaids while you're farther away. One bride more than fifty dollars in shipping and communications this way.

Shoes

〜 Comparison shop at different discount shoe stores and research the prices of the styles you see in the magazines. Check your local Marty's Shoes for quality choices. Also check your local sources for on-sale accessories.

〜 Visit dyeables.com to find pretty shoes in a range of prices and styles.

〜 Encourage your bridesmaids to wear pretty silver heels that they may already own rather than adding the expense of dyeing shoes.

> ## Order Shoes Together
>
> *Shoes, for the same reason as gowns, must be ordered in the same place. Differences in shoe colors among your maids can ruin your bridal party's look, so arrange to order as a group. The best way to do this is to pick out a shoe style at a national chain of shoe stores, get the style number from the clerk, and then ask your maids to go and try on that particular shoe in the same chain's stores near them. You know that a size seven in one style may be the same as a nine in another, so it's best to help your maids order shoes that will fit them correctly. Once the maids have their sizes in the style you've chosen, you can more accurately order their shoes for them.*

∽ Payless Shoes has a line of dyeable formal shoes as well.

∽ Encourage your maids to shop at shoe outlets (outlet bound.com) for a large discount on heels.

∽ Try for a group discount when you're ordering shoes to be dyed. Talk to the store manager about an order for six or more women. It's possible that your pair of shoes could be given to you free of charge if your order is large enough.

Rather than mailing the shoes to your maids, consider holding on to them at your house so your maids won't have to travel with bulky shoe boxes to your place for the wedding. Give the shoes to your maids a few days before the wedding so they can break them in and scuff the soles a bit to prevent slipping.

Shoes and Accessories

9 West—9west.com

Bloomingdale's—bloomingdales.com

Kenneth Cole—kennethcole.com

*Dyeables—dyeables.com

Fenaroli for Regalia—fenaroli.com

Kohl's—kohls.com (They have Vera Wang for less!)

Macy's—macys.com

Neiman Marcus—niemanmarcus.com

Payless—payless.com

Steve Madden—stevemadden.com

Target—target.com

Watters and Watters—watters.com

An asterisk (*) indicates companies with lower-priced merchandise options.

Accessories

⁓ Inexpensive gloves can be found at department stores if you want them. The ones that you see at bridal salons are probably overpriced, so check elsewhere first. If your wedding isn't a formal one, you may choose not to have your maids wear gloves.

⁓ Store-bought sashes can cost fifty dollars, so see if those bridesmaid dresses look beautiful enough without the waist-tied color contrast.

⁓ No need to spend a fortune on your bridesmaids' jewelry if that will be your gift to them. You'll find pretty silver sets at Target for less than fifteen dollars each, and they work very well for weddings!

Flower Girls

Dresses

⁓ Flower girl dresses at bridal salons are often overpriced, so avoid shopping there unless there's a mega-sale or trunk sale.

~ Their parents usually buy the flower girls' dresses, so do them a favor by suggesting an inexpensive style the little girls can use again.

~ Your flower girls can get a second wearing out of their First Communion or party dresses. Either leave the dresses unadorned or incorporate your color scheme through the use of ribbons, lace, a sash, or trim. For the price of just a fabric sash (eight dollars), flower girl Lauren's fancy white party dress became her dress for the wedding. She saved her family fifty-five dollars by not needing a new dress for that day.

~ Check out children's discount stores for your flower girls. You'll find a great variety of children's party dresses and more formal dresses, plus a wide selection of wedding-ready whites and pastels at post-Easter sales. Remember that plain white or off-white children's dresses can be dressed up to match your bridal party's colors.

~ Encourage the parents to check out outlet stores, with the help of outletbound.com, for the kids' outfits, shoes, and accessories.

~ Keep an eye out for department store sales, and pass along any coupons or sale notifications to the flower girls' parents.

∽ Have your flower girls' dresses made, either by a talented relative, a friend, or an inexpensive seamstress. Shop at fabric sales for the material. You won't need much. A smart shopper can assemble supplies for each flower-girl dress for thirty to forty dollars per dress.

Shoes

∽ Flower girls may wear their own party shoes or their dancing school ballet slippers for a free option.

∽ Get kids' party shoes at discount shoe stores or national discount chains such as Kohl's, Target, or Kmart. There's absolutely no need to get the flower girls' shoes at a bridal salon, no matter how pretty the styles.

Headpieces

∽ Wreaths of flowers look charming on the heads of flower girls, so consider this simple look for your wedding.

∽ Get pretty headbands or hair clips at an accessory store, Target, Kohl's, Wal-Mart, or other discount store for less than ten dollars each.

Accessories

~ Borrow a basket from a friend for each flower girl to carry during the ceremony. One bride saved the baskets that once held floral bouquets her fiancé had sent—double use and a good savings on extras.

~ Just like the bridesmaids, the flower girls' wedding day jewelry can come from Target for less than fifteen dollars. You don't need to give engraved jewelry anymore. Simple, wearable styles are more popular.

16

Dressing the Mothers of the Bride and Groom

No, you don't have to buy their gowns. You're just being a dutiful daughter (and daughter-in-law) by helping the mothers choose their best and most affordable look for your wedding day. Many brides like having a say in what the mothers wear, as it's lovely to have the moms in complementary colors and styles in the family wedding portraits.

$\mathcal{D}$resses

⁓ Look through magazines with your mother so the two of you can discuss which kinds of dresses will be appropriate and which colors you prefer. This way, you won't have to accompany your mother to every dress shop she wants to "just take a look in," and you won't have to fear her choice when she announces she's found the perfect dress. You'll also avoid her buying the wrong length of dress and having to get another one.

Coordinating the Mothers' Dresses
If the groom's mother lives far away from you or your mother, send her a swatch and a picture of the gown your mother has chosen so she can then make her selection. The mother of the bride chooses her dress first as an honor, and the mother of the groom should wear a similar but not identical style and a similar color. It looks better in the wedding photos if the mothers are in complementary rather than clashing colors.

~ Remember the mothers' dresses should adhere to the formality of your wedding. That means long gowns are out if the bridesmaids are wearing tea-length dresses. In essence, the mothers of the bride and groom are an extended part of the bridal party, so wardrobe rules apply to them as well. Besides, shorter, less formal gowns usually aren't as expensive as those floor-length, beaded numbers.

~ Avoid bridal salons for the mothers' dresses. As you know by now, prices here are often much higher than those of nonspecialized dress shops. Look in the formal section of a regular department store. Prices are bound to be lower than in the salon, and you may chance upon a sale. Identical gowns were seen in a bridal salon priced at $250 and at a regular dress shop for $175.

⌁ The mothers' gowns should be somewhat conservative in order not to outdo the bride's, and you will also avoid the extra expense of a flashier style.

⌁ Moms can shop from the prom gown racks as well! The styles are often elegant and sophisticated, and prices are often a fraction of traditional moms' gowns.

Compare and Save
Mom's gown in bridal salon $750
Mom's gown from bridesmaid's collection $125

⌁ Shop for mothers' gowns after major holidays. After-event overstock is reduced in price for clearance, often up to 60 percent.

⌁ Encourage moms to look on eBay for designer gowns.

~ Shop for the mother of the bride's and the mother of the groom's dresses in an outlet store for a considerable discount. You'll find savings up to 60 percent off or more in some national outlets.

~ Encourage moms to look in consignment shops for designer gowns at a fraction of the cost.

~ Buy a very simple gown in a department or discount store and add a jeweled neckline or fancy trim.

~ Moms can also shop at stores like Ann Taylor for well-priced gowns in their Occasions line.

Shoes

~ Avoid shoe selections at the bridal salon. They may be overpriced. Instead, comparison shop among the larger shoe chains in your area, at department stores, and at discount shoe stores.

~ Encourage the mothers to wear silver strappy shoes instead of having shoes dyed.

∼ Order the mothers' shoes with yours and your bridesmaids' for an even better group discount rate, if available. Remember to ask.

Accessories

∼ To save them money, encourage both mothers to wear their own jewelry and to forgo headpieces or hats.

17

Dressing the Men

Dressing the men, including the groom, groomsmen, fathers, and the little boys in the wedding party, can be quite pricey, with rentals averaging $50 to $150, new suits averaging $200, and designer shirts costing $50 or more. Here's how to help your men dress their best for less.

The Groom, Groomsmen, and Fathers of the Bride and Groom

∼ Research online to find out the best styles that suit the formality and location of the wedding, as well as the best-priced designers.

∼ Ask other recently married men where they shopped for their tuxes and suits. They did a lot of research and may be able to recommend the best places to go, as well as the places to avoid.

∼ Ask your wedding experts for their referrals as well. Vendors know each other and work together often, so they may be able to suggest a great tux shop. Some vendors offer partner coupons if you work with a tux shop they recommend. These coupons may get you 20 percent off.

Tuxedos or Suits

∼ Again, look at plenty of pictures in magazines and brochures to get an idea of the colors, fabrics, styles, and prices that suit your group best. Look at a picture of the tuxedo next to a picture of the bridesmaids' gowns. Make sure they look good together.

∼ Ask the tux shop clerk to show you different designers' lines in their budget collections.

∼ Always compare prices at tuxedo rental agencies around town. Prices vary according to which neighborhood they're in, if they're in a mall, if they're a chain, and so on.

∼ Look for a reputable tuxedo rental agency that offers group discounts.

∼ Ask if the groom gets his tuxedo free with your grooms-men's order or if the free tux can go to your father. This is usually offered standard at most tux shops if you order four or more tuxes.

∼ Order early, at least nine months in advance, to avoid rush fees.

∼ Know that prices are usually higher for the peak wedding season of May through September, as well as at prom time.

Getting Measurements

If the groomsmen and the fathers of the bride and groom are many miles away at the time of the tuxedo order, have the men send in their measurements on size cards so the correct tuxedos can be ordered for them. Be sure they get their measurements taken at a professional tailor's shop—again, no ruler and string job—so that the numbers are reliable.

〜 If the men will be wearing dark suits, their minor expense will be identical ties. Look in a discount store or at a department store sale for these.

Men's Formalwear Resources
After Hours—afterhours.com
Armani—armani.com (Check out Armani Exchange for
    discount lines.)
Bloomingdale's—bloomingdales.com
Brooks Brothers—brooksbrothers.com
Gingiss—gingiss.com
Hugo Boss—hugoboss.com
J Crew—jcrew.com
Lord & Taylor—lordandtaylor.com
Macy's—macys.com
Ralph Lauren—ralphlauren.com

〜 Visit outlet stores for men's suits, tuxedos, shirts, and more; see outletbound.com.

〜 Visit department stores during their winter holiday sales for more than 70 percent off all men's formalwear.

~ For less formal weddings, the men might wear khaki pants, crisp button-down shirts, and ties. Find these items at discount when stores like Eddie Bauer, Lands' End, and L.L.Bean have their big end-of-season and holiday sales. A fifty-dollar shirt may be on sale for nineteen dollars then.

Matching Pants Colors
Be careful of allowing men to wear khaki pants they already own. Khaki can range from tan to light green, so it's better to ask them all to buy their size in one style of new khaki pants. Tell them about sales and clearances so they can get bargains.

~ Make sure you get a signed copy of the contract or order receipt to verify your order in case of a mix-up. Record the style number, style name, sizes, deposit amount, check number, delivery date, and the name of the clerk who took your tuxedo order. Good record keeping ensures that any questions or mistakes made by the tuxedo agency can be cleared up quickly. Call several times to confirm the order and availability of the tuxedos—just to make sure.

~ If your groomsmen will be wearing dark suits instead of tuxedos, as in the case of an informal wedding, they may wear suits they already own. But just to be sure their look will be appropriate, arrange for the men to wear the suits ahead of time for you (perhaps to a dinner party). This way, you can check to see that their versions of dark are really dark, that the suits are in good order and style, and that leg and arm lengths aren't too short. Remember, you have a right to preview what the men will be wearing, so if they complain about the scrutiny, just tell them that the plans could be changed if they wish. They could always shell out the money for a tuxedo. You won't believe how quickly they'll have their suits tailored.

Shoes

~ Shoes can be rented at a group discount rate from the tuxedo rental shop.

~ The men in your wedding can purchase brand new shoes at a variety of outlet stores or discount shoe shops.

~ The men can wear their own dark shoes if dark suits will be their wedding day wardrobe. Again, arrange to see the shoes ahead of time.

$\mathcal{R}$ing Bearers

Suits

〜 If the ring bearer will be renting a tuxedo, try to get a discount at the store you've chosen as your men's outfitter. Most offer one-third off of boys' tuxedoes.

〜 Encourage parents to shop at kids' outlet stores for their suits and new shirts.

〜 Just like the groomsmen, search for sales on khaki pants or shorts, new button-down shirts, and ties at online outfitters.

〜 Boys' suits are on sale during First Communion time in April and May, and on deeper sale right after this time.

〜 Allow the ring bearer to wear his own suit, with a new bow tie to match the bridal party's color scheme.

Shoes

〜 Find a children's discount shoe store and look for an inexpensive style, or the ring bearer may wear a pair of his own dress shoes if they're appropriate.

18

Your Rings

Your wedding rings are the most lasting symbols of your wedding day and a statement of your personal style. While you shouldn't try to take too many shortcuts in saving on your bands, there are ways to get the best value and insure them for less.

Keep in mind that while all surveyed couples report checking the Internet for ring pricing, the vast majority are buying their rings in jewelry shops. The experience of trying on and buying rings is worth its weight in gold, and couples find that in-person shopping often nets them bigger discounts and the discovery of a more attractive, less expensive ring than they saw online.

Average Spending for Jewelry

	2008	2009	2010	2011	2012	2013
Engagement ring	$4,332	$4,459	$4,589	$4,723	$4,861	$5,003
Her ring	$902	$928	$955	$983	$1,012	$1,042
His ring	$569	$586	$603	$621	$639	$658

One hundred percent of couples polled research rings online, and 20 percent purchase online.

Printed with permission from TheWeddingReport.com.

Where to Find Your Rings

∽ Look in magazines or brochures to get an idea of the kind of rings you want. It's best to have a general idea before you walk into a jewelry store so you won't be swayed by the flashy choices in the display cabinet or by the commission-motivated salesclerk.

∽ Before you start your hunt, do some research on what to look for in quality gold and precious gem jewelry. Diamonds, for instance, are priced according to carat, color, clarity, and cut, with prices soaring the closer you get to perfection. So look at stones carefully, since a piece with slightly less clarity that you can't even see with the naked eye will be priced better.

〜 Ask friends and family where they shop for fine jewelry. You have to go for quality here, even if it means paying slightly more. You get what you pay for.

〜 Bring along a relative or friend who knows something about jewelry when you're shopping. You'll be more likely to ask the right questions.

〜 Ring stores in the mall may at times offer competitive prices during sales, such as before the winter holidays and before Valentine's Day and Mother's Day.

〜 For great deals on quality gems, shop in the diamond district of your nearest major city. This is where the buyers for all of those jewelry stores in the mall come to get wholesale prices and then sell the same jewels to you at higher prices. Check out where they're shopping, and you may discover a great find.

〜 Go to your family's regular jeweler for proven reliability and a possible discount for your loyalty to the place. One bride received 10 percent off on her rings just because she'd recently bought a gift there for her mother.

~ Comparison shop for your rings in different stores of different sizes, in different parts of town. Price tags vary, and you may be able to find a great deal.

~ Check department stores. Sales flyers will announce special savings, and throughout-the-store discounts may apply at the jewelry counter.

~ Visit Costco to see if their rings, at discount prices, meet your standards in quality. You might get a few hundred dollars off.

~ Visit a jewelry store's estate sale counter. Often these collections include valuable rings for hundreds of dollars off.

~ Are you traveling to an island where duty-free shopping means great prices on jewelry? Cruise ship passengers often disembark at St. Thomas, for instance, to net great discounts on fine jewelry. If you have a vacation coming up, consider a trip to an island for great shopping while you're there.

~ If you have a friend in the jewelry business, see if you can use his or her employee discount to garner a better price for your rings. This of course takes a good friend, who will be giving up a slice of commission on your purchase. It's worth a shot.

~ Visit discount jewelry websites like bluenile.com or zales
.com to find bargain prices and proven reliability with large
collections of rings.

~ Keep an eye out for sales, clearances, and specials. Ask your
family and bridal party to watch for specials in stores near them
as well. It could mean savings of 10 percent or more, which
could translate into a sizable discount. The pre-Christmas and
post–Valentine's Day sales offer amazing price cuts.

Check with the Better Business Bureau
*If the store isn't a large one, part of a national chain or well-
known line, check it out with the Better Business Bureau to see if
it's legitimate or if any charges have been leveled against it. A
ring purchase is a big-ticket item, so your best bet is to protect
your investment—even before you make it.*

~ Part of your criteria for choosing a ring shop is its engraving and sizing policies. If both are included free—and in some
places they aren't—it's an advantage. Measure this one carefully, though, because an expensive store with free sizing and
engraving is not better than an inexpensive store that charges
extra for engraving and sizing.

Ring Information and Company Websites

American Gem Society (for information on buying quality rings)—ags.org

Benchmark—benchmarkrings.com

Bianca—biancaplatinum.com

Blue Nile—bluenile.com

De Beers—adiamondisforever.com

EGL Gemological Society—egl.co.za

Fortunoff—fortunoff.com

Hearts on Fire—heartsonfire.com

Honora—honora.com

Jeff Cooper Platinum—jeffcooper.com

Lazare Diamond—lazarediamonds.com

Michael C. Fina—miachaelcfina.com

Novell—novelldesignstudio.com

OGI—ogi-ltd.com

Paul Klecka—klecka.com

Platinum Guild International USA—preciousplatinum.com

Scott Kay—scottkay.com

Tiffany—tiffany.com

Zales—zales.com

∽ Consider buying your rings in an antique shop, where beautiful rings with some history are offered at lower prices. Just be sure to get the rings appraised immediately to be sure you've gotten your money's worth. You may even find that your fifty-dollar ring is actually a valuable piece of jewelry.

Ring Designs

∽ No matter where you're ordering your rings, the choices you make can save you some money. Choose a set of plain rings over the swirly, gaudy ones that are larger than your whole hand. Another plus for smaller, simpler rings without texture and braiding is that they have no ridges to catch dirt, so they're easier to keep clean. For information on how to design your own rings, which could be a savings if you do it right, check out adiamondisforever.com.

∽ Buy plain metal bands rather than the kinds with the set stones. Keep in mind, though, that a top-name designer's plain gold ring is going to cost a lot more because of the brand. Always comparison shop to see if the plain, smooth band is indeed less expensive.

~ Learn about the prices of metal. Platinum is enjoying renewed popularity (see scottkay.com). But it is the most expensive precious metal, so be prepared to shell out thousands for a beautiful platinum ring. Most brides say it's worth the investment, and this is one place where you should not be cheap. You can get the same color effect with sterling silver or white gold for a fraction of the price. Visit bulliondesk.com to see how the prices of metals are doing on the stock exchange. These numbers do affect the price you'll pay.

Compare and Save

Platinum wedding band. $1,200

Similar wedding band in white gold. $600

~ Compare the prices of his and hers wedding band sets to the prices of individual rings. Only in that way can you decide which is the better buy. Some sets on sale can save you up to a hundred dollars off the price of individual rings.

~ For your wedding band, consider three- or five-diamond designs instead of eternity bands of diamonds all the way around.

〜 Look at rings with pave diamonds on top, a less expensive but still sparkly alternative to channel-set diamonds.

〜 Do you like the look of gemstones in your wedding band? Some precious gems are super-expensive (such as emeralds and rubies), but there are stones such as topaz and tsavorite that look like more expensive stones for a fraction of the price.

〜 You will see colored diamonds on the market, with yellow being among the most plentiful and thus less expensive than reds or blues.

〜 Beware of laser-cut rings with lots of detail, especially on men's rings where there's more metal to be covered and more work to be done.

〜 If your groom wants a thicker ring, go with white gold instead of platinum.

〜 If you know someone who makes jewelry as a hobby, commission that person to make your rings for you. No doubt the cost will be much lower than a store's, and your friend will be given a great honor. You also may design your own rings. Jillian found it special to actually help create her and her fiancé's wedding bands. She designed the rings, and then helped a friend make them. In doing so, she saved $450.

~ Put up flyers at a local art school or college with a jewelry workshop regarding your search for an artist to make a set of wedding rings. Students love these opportunities for their portfolios and independent study projects, and you'll undoubtedly get the ring for little more than the cost of materials. That can be more than half off store prices.

~ For the ultimate savings and meaning, exchange rings handed down to you by relatives. Keeping the bands in the family is important, and it's a special tie to those who have worn the bands before you.

~ Use one heirloom ring if you've fallen in love with it, and both of you can split the cost of the other, new ring.

~ Have the stones from an heirloom ring set in your wedding band. You save money on them, and the inclusion of your grandmother's diamonds in your ring is a very special gesture.

~ Buy stones separately from a discount supplier; then have them set into a ring you've gotten a bargain on elsewhere. The savings here are fifty to two hundred dollars.

〜 Jewelry stores often have loose stone sales. Get on their mailing list for special ring and stone events.

Important Shopping Tips to Protect Your Investment

〜 After you buy your rings, have them appraised immediately. Go to a jeweler other than the one from whom you bought the ring for this service. (Why would the salesclerk want you to know your ring isn't really worth the eight hundred dollars your fiancé spent?)

〜 Make sure your ring supplier offers a good return policy, in case you must exchange them for another size or style.

〜 Insure your rings right away.

〜 Learn how to care for your rings properly, to ensure a long life.

〜 Ask if the jewelry store does free ring fixes in the future. Many won't charge you to tighten a prong or polish your ring expertly.

19

Invitations and Save-the-Date Cards

Invitations, response cards, and programs can add up to a large part of your wedding budget. You can cut the expense without sending a cheap-looking, tacky invitation to your guests by knowing the details of the invitation-printing business and making the right selection. Remember, your invitations reflect the formality and style of your wedding, giving your guests an idea of what to expect and how to dress for the occasion. Design your invitation packages with that in mind, so you're not tempted to commit a faux pas by selecting the wrong invitation just to save money.

∽ The formality of your wedding is reflected in your invitations. So choose invitations that match the style of your wedding. Even formal invitations can be found for bargain prices.

Average Spending for Invitations and Stationery

	2008	2009	2010	2011	2012	2013
Invitations and reply cards	$431	$443	$456	$469	$482	$496
Personal stationery	$115	$118	$121	$124	$128	$132
Save-the-date cards	$156	$160	$165	$170	$175	$180
Thank-you cards	$72	$74	$76	$78	$80	$82

Ninety-six percent of couples polled research invitations and stationery online, and 57 percent purchase online.

Printed with permission from TheWeddingReport.com.

$\mathcal{K}$now What You Need

∼ Know exactly how many invitations you will need so you can comparison shop with the applicable numbers.

∼ When adding up the number of invitations you'll need, follow these rules: families get their own; those over the age of eighteen get their own; and those inviting a guest get one invitation with both names on it (no need for a separate invitation for the guest).

Invitation Resources

Invitations 4 Sale—invitations4sale.com

Anna Griffin Invitation Design—annagriffin.com

Birchcraft—birchcraft.com

Blue Tulip—bluetulip.com

Botanical PaperWorks—botanicalpaperworks.com

Carlson Craft—carlsoncraft.com

Crane and Co.—crane.com

Embossed Graphics—embossedgraphics.com

Envelopments—envelopments.com

Invitations by Dawn—invitationsbydawn.com

Julie Holcomb Printers—julieholcombprinters.com

Martha Stewart—marthastewart.com

Now and Forever—now-and-forever.com

PaperStyle.com—paperstyle.com

Papyrus—papyrusonline.com

The Precious Collection—preciouscollection.com

PSA Essentials—psaessentials.com

Renaissance Writings—renaissancewritings.com

Rexcraft—rexcraft.com

Vismara Invitations—vismarainvitations.com

Willow Tree Lane—willowtreelane.com

⌁ Plan to order ten to fifteen extras in case of mistakes or replacement guests added to the list when space allows. Leftovers may be kept as mementos.

Where to Shop

⌁ Shop around in several different stationery stores and at invitation websites to get the best prices available. Comparison shop like crazy to find the best prices.

⌁ Take several of those large invitation sample books home with you so you can take a really good look through them and compare prices. You'll want to experience textures, which you can't do with online images.

⌁ Visit invitations4sale.com for 40 percent off brand-name lines like Birchcraft and Carlson Craft, and a percent of your purchase is donated to the Leukemia and Lymphoma Society.

Choosing the Right Style

⌁ Choose thermographed invitations rather than engraved. You won't see much of a difference in style, but they're a much better buy. Linda Zec of An Invitation to Buy–Nationwide says thermographed invitations can cost up to 50 percent less than engraved ones.

~ Letterpress invitations are also growing in popularity for their inexpensive pricing.

~ Go with a simple and elegant design, perhaps with a pearl-ized border, rather than a super-embellished style that can cost twice as much.

~ Color is not usually an issue, so you will find comparable prices for pastel-shaded or brightly colored invitations.

~ Color *is* an issue when it comes to the color of ink you want your wording printed in. Choose from the company's standard ink colors that are included in the price and not from their premium list of designer colors. That standard dark green will look just as good as their hundred-dollar "evergreen" shade.

~ Choose from their standard fonts, using up to two different fonts per invitation design, and don't order their fancy-print, extra-charge fonts. It's just not worth wasting the extra money, and some fancier fonts are hard to read.

∿ Get regular- to small-sized invitations. They're less expensive than oversized ones, and extra postage is not needed for each one.

∿ Square invitations often cost more to mail, so precheck postage requirements before you order these trendy designs.

∿ Get plain envelopes. The colored ones with the printed and shiny liners are all decoration and all added expense.

∿ Choose invitations that are made of thinner paper so you'll pay less in postage. Those thick, cardboard-like invitations are just wasted money on two fronts: materials and mailing fees.

∿ The 100 percent cotton papers are the most expensive, so look for alternatives such as linen blends.

∿ Don't try to save a few dollars by not ordering response cards with your invitations. They're the best way to keep a record of how many guests will be in attendance at your wedding. You don't want to have to total up your guest list by calling all your relatives and friends.

∿ Recycled papers aren't always less expensive, so comparison shop to find the best paper stock for you.

$\mathcal{O}$rdering Wisely

~ Don't order your invitations too early—there may be a last-minute change of date, time, or place. Most brides do well to order their invitations four to six months in advance. By then, everything should be fairly well finalized.

~ When placing your order, print all information carefully, double-check, have your fiancé double-check, and then check again. Any mistakes you've made in the order will be printed on your invitation, and you'll be stuck with them.

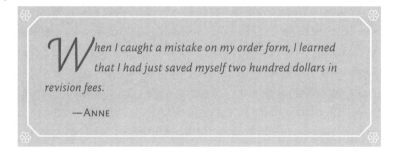

When I caught a mistake on my order form, I learned that I had just saved myself two hundred dollars in revision fees.

—ANNE

~ Make sure there's a return policy in your contract in case there is a mistake in the printing of the invitations or damage to your order in shipping.

~ Keep all receipts as proof of purchase, and get the sales-person's name when you place your order. Other information you should record: date of your order, specifics about the style and amount you're ordering, changes, delivery date, amount of deposit, and further payment obligations. These steps help in case of questions.

~ Check your invitations carefully when you go to pick them up. If you find mistakes right away, your chances are better for getting them corrected and compensated.

Making Your Own

~ Rather than order professional invitations from a printer or a catalog, you could choose to make your own, using good paper and your high-quality computer and printer. Today's paper and stationery stores stock a wide selection of beautiful bridal-themed invitation card stock, papers, and envelopes for you to use. Carefully follow the wording and patterns you see on invitations in wedding books and magazines, and enclose these in high-quality, matching envelopes with response cards.

~ Visit mountaincow.com for PrintingPress, an inexpensive invitation-design software, plus bargain-priced invitation papers and envelopes. You could create your entire invitation ensemble for less than fifty dollars.

~ Or, make use of a friend's computer skills and software. This favor can be your friend's wedding gift to you.

~ Buy your own white, off-white, or colored paper at office supply stores like Staples and Office Max for just a few dollars a ream, instead of buying fancier art papers for twenty dollars a ream.

~ Check out craft stores for inexpensive invitation card stocks and envelopes, using gift cards you requested as holiday and birthday gifts, making this *free*!

~ Check at Costco for inexpensive paper stock, printer inks, and envelopes.

~ Another alternative: use your computer to draw up the invitation you'd like, and bring a crisp printout to a nearby discount printer to be copied as many times as you need. You'll get top quality, and it usually turns out to be a big savings when you're not burning through three forty-dollar ink cartridges and putting wear and tear on your printer. Especially with big color graphics, the copies turn out better than ink-soaked home printings.

$\mathcal{C}$alligraphy

⮑ If you have experience in calligraphy, hand print a master copy of your invitation. Then either bring this master copy to a discount printer to be duplicated, or, if you have the time and patience, you can hand print all your invitations in calligraphy. It's a classy look if you have the talent, and it's more than a bargain.

Calligraphy Resources
Petals and Ink—petalsnink.com
Association for the Calligraphic Arts—calligraphicarts.org
(find referrals to local artists)

⮑ If you'd like the look of calligraphy for your invitations, ask an artist friend to write out your invitation as his or her gift to you. Or put up a flyer at a local high school or college art department, asking for the services of a calligrapher. Many young artists are just as talented as professionals, and they'd gladly do the job for a fraction of a professional's fee. They also use the work for their portfolios.

~ Professional calligraphers charge substantial fees for their work, so if you must hire out the job, comparison shop for the best talent at the right price.

Compare and Save

Professional calligrapher . . . . $300 and up

Do it yourself. . . . . $25 for supplies

A friend's gift to you. . . . . free

~ Check out the calligraphy fonts on your home computer. You might already have easy and free access to terrific font styles you don't even know about. Try the following in Microsoft Word: Century Schoolbook, Edwardian Script, Fine Hand, French Script, Goudy Old Style, Lucida Fax, Vivaldi, and Vladimir Script.

$\mathcal{S}$ending Out Invitations

~ Mail the invitations early enough so that the response cards will be returned to you several weeks before you have to give the final head count to the caterer. A delay or change could cost you money.

> **Postal Service Online**
>
> *To save time and make sure your invitations reach your guests, visit the U.S. Postal Service's website at usps.gov to find out zip codes. Don't order stamps here, though. Buy in person at the post office to save on shipping costs.*

~ Be sure you have all your guests' names and addresses correct so no invitations are returned to you, leaving an irate aunt who thinks she has been snubbed.

~ Don't use printed labels to address your invitations. It's tacky and a waste of money. Address them by hand for the classiest look.

At-Home Cards

～ Separate cards to announce your permanent address, phone number, and even the name you'll be assuming (whether it's his, yours, or a hyphenated combination) are one of those nonessentials that can easily be cut to keep your wedding and postage costs down, especially if your guests already know where you'll be living. This information can be printed on the back of your wedding program.

Thank-You Notes

～ Rather than order these with your invitations as part of your stationery package, simply use a high-quality plain stationery (not necessarily thank-you or bride's stationery), and handwrite your thank-you in black ink. Comparison shop among discount stationery stores for the best price, taking care to look at price-per-card cost.

～ Don't buy bridal thank-you notes at a bridal shop. They're higher priced in any bridal store.

~ Visit invitations4sale.com for 40 percent off thank-you notes.

~ Don't use those boxed, fill-in-the-blank thank-you cards. They're not only expensive, they're tacky.

Maps and Printed Directions

~ If you're planning to send maps to your guests who might need help finding the ceremony site and the location of the reception, include the directions with the invitation. Many hotels and reception halls provide printed maps and directions to their sites. In most cases, these thorough direction sheets are free for the asking.

~ Copy your map or directions on a photocopier—yours, a friend's, or the one at work—any one you can use for free. An added tip: reduce these maps so you can fit two to four to each page. Then copy these sheets at less of a strain on paper or supplies or on your cash supply if you have to pay to use a copier.

~ Visit weddingmapper.com to create a free, personalized map that you can e-mail to your guests or print out to enclose in their welcome baskets.

 ∿ Of course, send maps only to those guests who need them, as well as to your vendors.

Save-the-Date Cards

Save-the-date cards announce your impending wedding plans to guests by sharing your wedding date, the location it will be held, and the URL of your personal wedding website.

 ∿ Visit a discount invitation website such as invitations4 sale.com and look among the least expensive collections. You'll often find the smaller, less ornate cards to be elegant and sophisticated, and they cost half as much as the more colorful, graphic ones.

 ∿ Visit vistaprint.com to order design-them-yourself save-the-date postcards for less than ten dollars. This website often offers *free* postcards with your order of save-the-date cards, saving you even more money. One bride reports that she took advantage of a Vistaprint holiday sale where all postcards were free, and she only had to pay shipping. She got her entire save-the-date card order for $6.45. If she had ordered from a regular invitation site, they would have cost $120.

∼ Use hallmark.com to send free save-the-date messages written into their online, interactive greeting cards for the majority of your guests, and for any guests who do not have e-mail, simply handwrite the announcement on a note card you have at home (or a store-bought note card) and mail it to them. We're still in an age when many of our grandparents and great-aunts and -uncles haven't gotten on board with e-mail, and it's most polite to send them their own announcements rather than expect their kids and grandkids to tell them about the upcoming wedding.

∼ You can also use the "Share Your Site" feature of your personal wedding website as a free save-the-date message when you word the notification e-mail with your excited announcement.

∼ You can skip save-the-date cards if you plan to mail your wedding invitations twelve weeks in advance, rather than the traditional six to eight weeks, to give your guests plenty of notice, allowing them to book any airfare without rush fees, and so on.

20

Destination Weddings

A growing number of brides and grooms are choosing to have destination weddings with just a handful of guests, instead of one hundred or more guests in a hometown wedding, as a way to both save money and plan a unique, exciting getaway where they can marry in tropical splendor. The resort industry has created phenomenal destination wedding packages with many free perks for the bride and groom, so you have many opportunities for savings. All of the tips in this book apply to destination weddings, since you will be choosing menus and flowers and gowns, and travel is a factor. So read on to find out more ways to save, specifically targeted to your destination wedding.

⁓ Ask recently married friends where they went for their destination wedding. Even if you choose the same location, since you just heard how terrific it was and how budget-friendly it was, those guests will love revisiting the site of their own wedding.

≈ Research destination wedding packages and resorts online, through your travel agent, and at destinationbride.com, where many of the great destinations are reviewed by a wedding coordinator who has planned weddings in those locales.

≈ Choose a destination that will be in its shoulder season at the time of your wedding. The shoulder season is the period of time just after peak season and right before the "off-season." Since the weather is often still ideal, resort amenities and attractions are all still open, their full-time regular staff is on hand, and you have every feature of an in-season visit at a lower price. (In the off-season, many locals close their shops or scale back their hours.)

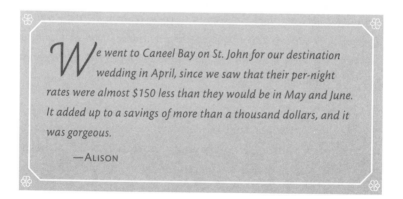

We went to Caneel Bay on St. John for our destination wedding in April, since we saw that their per-night rates were almost $150 less than they would be in May and June. It added up to a savings of more than a thousand dollars, and it was gorgeous.

—ALISON

~ Visit travelandleisure.com to see their World's Best resorts and islands, particularly the best budget-priced resorts and destinations.

~ Investigate each resort's destination wedding packages to see what else might be included. Many offer a free honeymoon to the bride and groom if they bring more than twenty guests with them for the wedding. That can be a savings of a few thousand dollars. Other freebies in the competitive world of destination wedding packages may include free rentals of kayaks and snorkeling gear, free spa treatments, a free dinner for all, and other perks.

~ Ask about discounted rates on meal plans for your group. The sales manager may be able to give you the same 15 percent off that they give corporate groups. You just have to ask.

~ Ask about group discounts for airline fare as well. Many airlines now offer 10 to 20 percent off group fares as a way to entice wedding groups to book with them and not with competitors.

~ Sign up for a honeymoon registry and include spa treatments, dinner cruises, golf rounds, or just gift cards to the resort so that your friends and family can contribute to some elements of your wedding. A gift card to the hotel spa could pay for your wedding day hairstyle.

∽ Use the resort's own experts instead of trying to find and communicate with vendors at the destination on your own. Some resorts won't allow outside vendors on their grounds, so be wary of booking independently, since you may lose your deposits (and experience chaos) when you find out at a late date that your pros can't participate.

∽ Limit the floral decor for your ceremony and reception. Most resorts are already so beautiful, with great natural scenery and flowers on the grounds, that you don't need to do anything else.

∽ Buy your dress at home, instead of on the island. Some resorts offer designer lines of destination-style wedding dresses, but those can be pricey and are intended for people who wish to spontaneously marry or renew their vows while on the island. You don't want to pay more because those gowns are the only ones available to you.

∽ Rather than plan wedding weekend events such as cocktail parties and sporting tournaments for pay, allow your guests to have their own downtime on each day. Most people attend destination weddings as their vacations, so you don't need to overbook them (for a big price). Provide your guests with a list of free amenities such as the resort's gym or snorkeling gear before the getaway so that they can plan their own itineraries.

~ It's good form to provide your destination wedding guests with a great welcome basket containing sunscreen, hiking maps, snacks and bottled water, perhaps a small bottle of rum or other liquor, and a gift card to the hotel gift shop for any essentials they need to pick up. You can create this basket for less than thirty dollars by shopping at home, not at the destination.

~ Consider purchasing travel insurance to protect your getaway and wedding in case of a storm or other disaster. Insurance plans might cost two hundred dollars or so, but they're worth the money to allow you to redo your big event if needed.

21

Flowers and Decorations

Brides who have tried too hard to save money in this area report that they regretted settling for less than they wanted for their wedding day. You don't have to shortchange your floral vision for the sake of saving money. Here you'll find out how to get more for your flower budget by making the right choices according to style, season, and selection.

Check First!

~ Check with the officiant or the manager of the site of the wedding. Will the location be decorated already? If so, you have much less to buy. One bride learned that her church would be decorated already with poinsettias and white candles on the date of her pre-Christmas wedding. This saved her five hundred dollars in extra florist fees.

〜 Another reason to check with the officiant at a church or synagogue is to inquire about rules regarding decoration. You may not be allowed to set up pew arrangements, and it would be unfortunate to find this out after you paid seventy-five dollars for yours. You should get the dos and don'ts before you start ordering.

〜 See if there will be other weddings taking place at your wedding location on the same day as yours. Perhaps you could arrange through the officiant or manager to share basic decorations with the other bride or brides at a savings to all of you. Emily asked the officiant to give her name to the other bride, who then contacted her. They saved three hundred dollars by splitting the costs of decorating their church.

〜 Set a budget for your flowers, using the figures you've discovered through introductory research or talks with recently married friends, and stick to it. Visit costofwedding.com to see what the average floral budget is in your zip code, just to get an idea of the range near you.

Average Spending for Flowers

	2008	2009	2010	2011	2012	2013
Boutonnieres/corsages	$169	$174	$179	$184	$189	$194
Bride bouquet	$146	$150	$154	$158	$163	$168
Bridesmaid bouquets	$232	$239	$246	$253	$260	$267
Ceremony flowers	$428	$440	$453	$466	$479	$493
Flower girl flowers	$48	$49	$50	$51	$52	$53
Reception flowers	$1,010	$1,039	$1,069	$1,100	$1,132	$1,164

Printed with permission from TheWeddingReport.com.

$\mathcal{W}$*here to Look*

∼ Don't go to a big, fancy florist connected to a bridal salon, a mall, a hotel, or even a caterer. Their elevated prices mean you're also paying for their rent, their facilities, their advertising, and their larger staff. Instead, look at a more moderate supplier.

∼ Use your family's regular florist because you're sure of their reliability and quality of service. You may even get a discount for being a regular customer. Karen received a 20 percent discount on her wedding flowers from her regular florist, plus another 10 percent off because the same florist also did her sister's wedding.

~ Check floral wholesaler shops in your area, which are sometimes found in floral centers in large cities or as storefronts and nurseries elsewhere. Their prices are by nature lower than those you'll find in other stores and markets. You'll find listings of these online.

~ Comparison shop at several different florists and nurseries in several different parts of town. Prices may vary depending on neighborhood, access, size of facilities, and type of clientele.

~ A shop that grows its flowers and plants on-site is generally less expensive than the shop that has to have all of its blooms shipped in. The high cost of fuel means many vendors are hiking up their prices to cover their deliveries. So look for greenhouse or gardening space around the shops you're checking out.

~ Ask your nearby friends and relatives if they would suggest a florist whose service they like. Use that information when you're comparing prices and packages.

～ Find a young, just-starting-out-in-the-business florist who will give his or her all. Most often, these beginners lack experience, not talent, and their reasonable prices are meant to attract accounts that will give them valuable exposure and graphics for their websites. Tracy found a great new florist at considerable savings when a hardworking newcomer distributed flyers in her neighborhood. So don't count out the beginners. You just might get a great deal, and you might get access to the newest training and trends that were taught to this beginner at the floral design school he or she just attended. A longtime pro might still be using old or outdated techniques and a smaller range of flowers due to a lack of new training.

～ When comparison shopping at floral suppliers, review their brochures and sample albums and ask to see arrangements they're working on now. Note their prices and the elements of their packages so that you can compare and contrast all the possibilities.

～ Take a look at online floral wholesalers such as freshroses .com and onlinewholesaleflowers.com and you might find big price breaks on flowers you'll arrange yourself.

*S*mart Shopping

When ordering, keep the following things in mind to save yourself some money.

~ Get a price comparison chart for each of the flowers you might want to include in your bouquets and decorations. This way, you'll be able to see which blooms are most and least expensive, and you can choose the most economical ones. Lilies, carnations, and freesia, for example, are far less costly choices than the popular stephanotis and orchids.

~ You don't have to buy the cheapest flowers available. According to Marilyn Waga of Belle Fleur in New York City, "Use a few great, eye-catching flowers in each arrangement, rather than a lot of unimpressive, cheap flowers." Great, beautiful blooms can be just as lovely as a bunch of roses, and it will make your bouquet more original.

~ Order baby roses instead of big Ecuadorian roses and other varieties for a savings of 10 to 20 percent. Roses are plentiful throughout the year, so you *can* use them in your floral pieces without damaging your wedding budget too much.

∾ Use the florist's chart as well to find out which flowers have to be flown in. Shipping an exotic selection of flowers will be more expensive than using those found closer. Stephanotis needs to be flown in, since it's grown in Hawaii, as is bird-of-paradise. Visit theflowerexpert.com for great articles on exotic flowers, as well as locally grown blooms for your area.

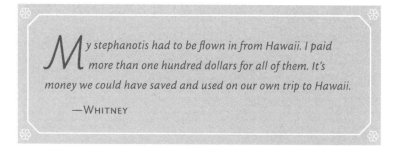

My stephanotis had to be flown in from Hawaii. I paid more than one hundred dollars for all of them. It's money we could have saved and used on our own trip to Hawaii.

—WHITNEY

∾ Use traditional wedding flowers sparingly, especially during the most popular wedding months like June and September. White roses, stephanotis, gardenias, and orange blossoms are more expensive then.

∾ Inexpensive flowers that work well in any floral arrangement are ivy (which symbolizes wedded bliss), zinnias in bright colors, tulips in season, leatherleaf, and Queen Anne's lace.

〜 Order flowers that are in season. Just like fruits and vegetables, prices go up when it's not their prime time. Your florist can tell you what will be in season on your wedding day, depending on where you live. It's a very important question to ask, since some flowers triple in price when they're not readily available.

In-Season Flowers
- **Spring wedding flowers:** anemone, bells of Ireland, Casa Blanca lily, daffodil, delphinium, hyacinth, lilacs, narcissus, peony, ranunculus, star gazer lily, sweet pea, tulip
- **Summer wedding flowers:** alstroemeria, bells of Ireland, chrysanthemum, English lavender, forget-me-not, freesia, gerbera daisy, hydrangea, iris, larkspur, lily, lisianthus, Queen Anne's lace, snapdragons, stephanotis, stock, sunflowers, tuberose, yarrow, zinnia
- **Fall wedding flowers:** aster, chrysanthemum, dahlia, marigold, zinnia
- **Winter wedding flowers:** amaryllis, anemone, bells of Ireland, camellias, Casa Blanca lily, cosmos, daffodil, forget-me-nots, holly, jasmine, narcissus, poinsettia, ranunculus, star gazer lily, star of Bethlehem, sweet pea, tulip
- **Wedding flowers available year-round:** baby's breath, bachelor's button, calla lily, carnations, delphinium, eucalyptus, gardenia, gladiolus, heather, lily of the valley, orchid, rose, scabiosa

〜 Order miniature flowers rather than the full-sized variety. Not only are they more delicate, they may be priced at a fraction of the cost—depending on the particular flower.

〜 Consider sprays, which have several flowers per sprig. One spray can give the appearance of several three-dollar flowers.

〜 Use color in your bouquets and arrangements. A splash of color gives the impression of more flowers in the bunch, and you won't have to buy as many flowers to make a statement as if you used all-white arrangements.

〜 Use more greenery in your bouquets and decorations. The natural look is in, so include plenty of ferns and pretty leaves to fill out a bouquet with fewer flowers.

Bouquets

〜 Consider filling out your bouquets and decorations with Queen Anne's lace or similar inexpensive blooms that give a delicate, romantic impression.

〜 Be sure the shape of your bouquet fits your height and size. A short bride looks hidden behind a too-large bouquet, so avoid ordering a more expensive style that isn't right for you.

Hold different-sized circular items such as a paper plate and a Frisbee in front of you to gauge the perfect circle of flowers to suit your frame. You can then show that size to your florist to design a bouquet that may be smaller—and less expensive— than the florist was planning to create for you.

~ Remember that the main cost of a bouquet is in its composition. A super-detailed bouquet style is going to take more time to create than a hand-tied style where stems are gathered together and wrapped.

Compare and Save

Detailed Biedermeyer bouquet.........................$250

Hand-tied bouquet.....................................$80

Single-stem flower, wrapped with ribbon ....under $10

~ Big bouquets are out, since brides want their gowns to be in the spotlight. Plus, big bouquets are heavy to carry around. Go smaller and thus less expensive. A top trend now is for brides to carry nosegay bouquets, which can cost half as much as a traditional bouquet.

～Carry a collection of cut roses, tulips, daisies, or calla lilies, hand tied and wrapped with satin ribbon up the length of the stem. This pretty, classic look costs one-third the price of a traditional round bouquet, and brides love how light it is.

～ A popular inexpensive trend for outdoor weddings: carry a cluster of wildflowers for less than twenty dollars.

～ Another popular budget choice for brides who want to show off their gowns: carrying a single flower such as an oriental or stargazer lily for less than five dollars. This look is popular at garden and outdoor weddings, destination weddings, and even at formal evening weddings with a dramatic red flower set against a white dress. It's a budget victory!

～ Order a much smaller bouquet for the one you'll toss to the waiting single women at your reception. There is no rule that says it has to be identical to your real one. Or you could just toss your own bouquet if you're not planning to preserve it and keep it as a memento of your day. Also, the bouquet toss is falling out of fashion, so you may want to skip ordering a nosegay.

～ Order smaller versions of your bouquet for your brides-maids to carry. Theirs can be two-thirds the size of yours and cost two-thirds as much.

～ Use less expensive flowers in your bridesmaids' bouquets. All-rose bouquets without the callas, gardenias, and stephan-otis will cost you one-third less, if not one-half less.

～ Bridesmaids can carry single-stemmed roses or calla lilies with the stem tied with ribbon for less than five dollars in some cases!

～ Bridesmaids can carry a hand-tied collection of calla lilies, daisies, or tulips for less than twenty dollars. The easy compo-sition of a hand-tied bouquet reduces the price.

Mothers' Flowers

～ Corsages to be worn by the mothers and grandmothers don't have to be very large. In fact, most women prefer a smaller corsage to wear on the wedding day. Check if corsages worn on the wrist are less expensive than the pin-on variety at your floral designer's.

~ Moms can carry small nosegays or single flowers tied at the stem with pretty ribbons instead of wearing a corsage for less than ten dollars.

$\mathcal{D}$elivery

~ Bypass the delivery fee by picking up your order from the florist yourself. You could save twenty-five to fifty dollars, depending on the size of your order. Make sure you have plenty of insulated coolers and a few sturdy boxes so that your flowers will arrive fresh and uncrushed at the wedding.

~ Of course, if you'll be picking up the flowers yourself, you'll want to arrange to do it at the last possible time before the ceremony. It could be a morning run after breakfast, or you could send someone from your bridal party to take care of this for you. Decorating the ceremony and reception locations with these freshly picked-up supplies is a wedding morning task that might be best handled by a less nervous bridal attendant or helpful friends and relatives.

Ceremony Flowers

〜 You can decorate your own chuppah with flowers and garlands you order from a wholesaler. A floral designer could decorate it for you, but those flowers and labor time can add up to hundreds of dollars. See if you can use a chuppah your site already owns for free, rather than renting it . . . as a perk you'll ask for when you book your wedding at that site.

〜 Instead of ordering rose petals to be strewn about by the flower girl during the ceremony, gently pull the petals off several roses from your garden. One bride who followed this tip saved seventy-five dollars on her florist bill.

〜 Before ordering a white aisle runner from your florist, check to see if the church or wedding location has one, or simply skip the aisle runner. You'll look better in contrast with a darker floor rather than blending with a white path. An off-white dress will look better, too, without the white clash underfoot.

〜 If your wedding falls in the right season, cut evergreens from your Christmas tree before you discard it. Unsold Christmas trees may be purchased after the season for a minimal price. Use the branches as centerpiece additions if they're not dried out. Or buy a fresh tree in-season for a hundred dollars and cut it up to create garlands and decor that would otherwise cost you several hundred dollars if ordered from a floral designer.

∾ If your wedding location is already nicely decorated, you could skip the pew decorations. If your first several rows need to be reserved with some kind of markers, use lengths of ribbon instead of decorations. Craft stores offer inexpensive pew bow kits for less than ten dollars.

Reception Decor

∾ Use candelabras or candleholders from your home. If you were to rent these for several tables, you could spend anywhere from fifty to seventy-five dollars.

∾ Use potted plants from home or borrow potted plants and flowering bushes from friends and family to decorate a small reception space.

∾ Buy your centerpieces as investments in your future home. Home Depot's selection of potted flowers are often less than ten dollars each, and they guarantee their plants 100 percent.

Also look there for topiaries in pretty clay pots that can be set out on each table. After the wedding have a friend bring them back to your house to use as home or garden decor. Mike and Stephanie used their wedding shower gift cards to Home Depot—where they were registered—to buy twenty potted flowers for their centerpieces for two hundred dollars. Home Depot and Lowes are great sources of wedding day flowers.

∽ If you want flowers rather than greenery, here's a great secret shared by a bride in Kentucky: go to your local supermarket and raid its flower section of all the potted flowering plants. This bride bought thirty potted plants for ninety dollars and kept the colored foil paper on the flowerpots for a bright look.

∽ Go to Costco for terrific bargains on floral bouquets and single-stem flowers, potted flowers, and small potted plants to use as your decor . . . all for half of what you'd pay at a floral designer's studio. You will have to shop no sooner than the day before the wedding and use whatever you find in stock, but it's still a great way to save.

∽ Check Whole Foods Market (wholefoods.com) for their organic flowers, greenery, and plants. Many florists say this is where they get their floral supplies, so if the pros go there for bargains, so should you.

∼ Cut branches from flowering trees to use as decoration for your tables, buffet tables, and the altar. Again, this must be done shortly before the ceremony so your blooms aren't wilting and discoloring. Keep the cut branches cool and their angle-cut stems in water. Of course, make sure these are *your* flowering trees, such as the group of cherry trees in your backyard, and that you don't kill the trees with overzealous cutting.

∼ Buy candles in bulk from discount stores, craft supply houses, even catalogs. And freeze them before using them—they'll last much longer.

∼ For a head table or buffet table, use a good tablecloth from home rather than renting one.

*C*enterpieces

There really is no need for expensive florist-created centerpieces. Oversized ones obstruct your guests' view of one another (and you) anyway, and a pretty centerpiece doesn't necessarily have to have a large price tag attached. Here are some inexpensive and tasteful alternatives to the tabletop jungle.

∼ Have your florist create low-set bunches of tulips or ranunculus in glass vases for one-third the cost of large floral centerpieces.

∼ Arrange candles of different heights to create a romantic look for each table. Remember to freeze the candles first so they will burn more slowly.

∼ Set in the center of each table groups of framed pictures of you and your fiancé together, with family, with friends, as children, and so on. Use frames and pictures you've taken from your own walls and countertops, and recruit both families to bring theirs in as well. (Ask them to stick an address label on the backs of their frames for easier return after the party.) One bride found that her guests loved looking at the photos on the table; they were appreciated far more than one hundred dollars' worth of floral centerpieces would have been.

∼ Float miniature candles along with flower petals in a large water-filled glass bowl at the center of each table. Find glass bowls in bulk at craft stores for three to five dollars each, and order loose flowers from your florist or wholesaler.

∼ Arrange a fruit bowl at the center of each table or place a larger one as the centerpiece of a buffet table. Search farmer's markets and supermarkets for the best quality and prices available, or ask the reception hall manager if the fruit from the buffet table might be arranged this way for free.

~ A large bread basket makes a great centerpiece, especially if you include braided breads and a variety of shapes, sizes, and colors. Again, ask the caterer if you'd be able to use the bread intended for the buffet table for this purpose. Use your own pretty baskets or borrow them. If baskets are not available to you, simply cover any kind of bowl with a large cloth napkin and have it drape over the bowl once it's filled with rolls. (In days long ago, grain was considered a symbol of fertility, and the bride and groom were showered with grain for that very reason. In other cultures of the past, bread was a gift brought by all and arranged in one pile. This is thought to be the origin of the wedding cake.)

~ Neatly arranged groups of wedding favors also make nice centerpieces. Why not get double duty out of your favors and save some money at the same time?

~ Check markets, sales, even your attic for items you can use as centerpieces. A brass theme will allow you to dig up all sorts of interesting things.

⌁ Choose creative centerpieces rather than floral arrangements. For a holiday wedding, set out pretty bowls or silver trays filled with a selection of your holiday ornaments. For a beach wedding, fill a small fishbowl with sand, some seashells, and dried starfish.

Consider the following ideas if you're not the do-it-yourself type but want the do-it-yourself savings.

⌁ Contact a floral design college or school to request their services as a group project for pay. The instructor will surely jump at your offer, and you'll wind up paying much less than you would to a commercial business. The quality is often outstanding, as these students are fresh in their knowledge of technique and the rules of design.

⌁ Accept the services of an experienced relative or friend as his or her wedding gift to you.

⌁ Find centerpiece bowls on the cheap at your local craft store.

⌁ To fill your hall or tent with lights, ask your relatives if you can borrow their strings of white Christmas lights. Label each string with the lender's name, and then use all of the strings together to create a lovely, starry look for your site.

〜 Since stones are a big trend for wedding centerpieces, especially if dotted with a few flowers, go to Home Depot or Lowes and buy a big bag of river stone or "egg" stones, wash them well, and divide them for use in each centerpiece bowl.

〜 Watch out for metal prices when it comes to finding centerpiece vases and bowls. Silver mint julep cups became almost impossible to find, and very expensive, when silver prices rose. So look at pretty tin bowls and vases that *look* like silver.

〜 Don't order glass centerpieces from bridal websites, since you'll pay extra for shipping and lose any discount you may find. Always go to the craft store to choose from their bulk supplies . . . you'll often find the very same round and rectangular glass vases there!

〜 Check the dollar store for their collection of small glass centerpiece vases.

〜 Ask your floral designer if you can use his or her collection of leftover centerpiece bowls. Floral designers often have a basement or storage room filled with silver or glass vases they didn't use from other weddings they worked, and even if they don't match exactly in style, the all-silver or all-glass theme will work!

⌁ Ask if your reception site has elevated centerpiece holders in wrought iron, or their own vases, that you can use for free. Many sites keep their own collections, and you can use them if you ask. Your savings: more than two hundred dollars.

22

Transportation for All

The most important thing on the wedding day is actually getting to the ceremony and reception. You will want to arrive and depart in style, so learn here how to book transportation for less and avoid extra fees that can wreck a budget.

Average Spending for Transportation						
	2008	2009	2010	2011	2012	2013
Car rental	$257	$265	$273	$281	$290	$299
Limo rental	$690	$711	$732	$754	$777	$800

Printed with permission from TheWeddingReport.com.

For the Bride and Groom

~ When looking for limousines, always comparison shop. Prices vary wildly, and many companies offer special packages and discounts. Make plenty of calls and take plenty of notes. Of course, you'll need to know your wedding date when you start looking for a limo company—some agencies may not have any limousines available on your wedding day. Visit costof wedding.com to see what couples in your area are spending on transportation.

~ Never contract with a limousine agency with just a phone call. Always go to see the cars. You want to be sure you won't wind up with an old red model with a worn interior and no air-conditioning—their version of "deluxe."

~ Book a quality limousine company that's close to your locations. Your time starts when they leave the lot, so you'd otherwise pay a lot extra for their driving time before they even get to you.

~ Figure out how many cars you really need. One limousine company owner told me that he regularly has to decrease couples' estimates of the number of cars needed to transport their guests. Don't forget that some limousines seat eight, some seat ten, and some seat twelve or more.

〜 When adding up the number of limousines needed, you can cut costs tremendously by just getting one for yourselves. After all, the bridal party doesn't have to be transported in limos.

〜 Choose a regular, not a stretch, limousine for the two of you. The look is the same, but the price is lower.

〜 Choose a black limousine rather than a white one. White limos are far more expensive than the standard black ones, which give you a better deal and more availability when shopping for your wedding day ride.

〜 Pass on the special bridal package that includes a complimentary bottle of champagne for the bride and groom. Most brides who paid for this type of package said either the champagne wasn't very good or the church and reception hall were so close that they didn't have any time to drink the champagne. Just a plain old ride in the car will do.

〜 Ask for the free extras that are now becoming standard in the transportation industry: red carpet leading up to the car door; champagne stand for a post-ceremony champagne toast by the car; water, ice, and snacks stocked in the limousine. Don't allow a company to charge you extra for any of these items. They're free at most reputable companies.

〜 Be sure to schedule your time wisely. If you keep the limousine driver waiting outside the reception hall for you to leave the party—and you've stayed an hour longer than you planned to because you were having so much fun—you could wind up paying the driver for the extra time plus overtime. Some companies charge $150 to $200 an hour for overtime! One bride and groom in this situation wound up paying the limo company two hundred dollars in extra fees. Ask about time arrangements and extra fees.

〜 Get a contract written up with all the details of your agreement, including the number of cars you'll need, where and when each of them is to report, deposits, and the signature or name of the person who took your reservation. Again, this is a larger expense, so you'll want to protect your investment. Plus, if one of the three limousines you've hired to transport the bridal party doesn't show up, you have proof that you're entitled to a partial refund.

～ Just book the limousine for a ride from your ceremony to your reception for less than one hundred dollars. Bridal party members can transport both you and your groom to the ceremony in their own cars, perhaps decorated with fun, inexpensive wedding-themed magnets from the party supply store. Or just schedule individual drop-offs and pickups instead of the five-hour wedding package.

～ If friends or relatives have special connections at a limousine company, ask if they might be able to get you a discount. Perhaps they could consider it their wedding present to you.

～ Don't have the limo wait for you through the reception. Arrange for a separate ride to your hotel or home. This saves you five to six hours of limo on-the-clock time, often five hundred dollars or more.

Limousines aren't the only way to travel. Look into other forms of transportation.

～ Book a luxury sedan rather than a limousine. These cars are just as sleek and special, some with tinted windows for a little privacy. Be sure to ask for the newest model and contract for the car to be washed and waxed right before your big day. One couple tried to save by hiring a sedan, which showed up dirty and covered with salt from its previous long rides on winter roads.

$\sim$ Compare prices at car rental agencies—especially those that offer luxury or exotic cars. It might be cheaper to rent a convertible or even an Excalibur for an hour (to the ceremony and reception only), rather than a limo.

$\sim$ Check out classic and antique car associations for prices and availability. In most cases you can make your getaway in a classic that says more about your personalities than a standard limo, and the prices are often much less expensive.

$\sim$ Look online at cona.org, the Carriage Operators of North America, to find special transportation such as horse and carriage rides. Research these carefully, and always go to see the horse and carriage. Consider here, though, the traffic in your area. Will this horse and carriage have to cross a four-lane highway to get to the reception? The conditions may not be right for a horse and carriage transport, and distance is a factor, but you might find the ideal package and locale.

$\sim$ If you live close to the ceremony and the reception, consider a walking procession from place to place. On a comfortable day, your parade will be great fun for everyone and the center of attention. Older or disabled guests can be driven the short distance, of course.

~ Enlist the help of a friend who has a nice car, possibly a convertible. With this free option at your disposal, you're more likely to be able to decorate this car with streamers and "Just Married" signs than you are with a rented car or limousine.

~ Have your parents or honor attendants drive you to and from the airport for your honeymoon. It's much smarter than hiring a limo, you don't have to worry about a waiting limousine driver and a ticking clock, and you get a better welcome home.

For the Bridal Party

~ Of course, limousines for the bridal party aren't a necessity, but if you wish to provide them you should comparison shop among limousine companies. Since you most likely will be renting more than one limo, see if you can get a group rate.

> **Don't Crowd the Limousine**
> *Don't attempt to cram ten people into one limousine.*
> *Remember the women's dresses shouldn't be crushed and*
> *wrinkled by overcrowding in a car. Consider adequate space*
> *while tallying cars.*

∼ Have helpful relatives and friends drive the bridal party around in their nice cars—cleaned, of course. Convertibles are fun for the celebrating group, so offer your car as well if you have one.

∼ If you have a large bridal party, don't book four or five limos to haul them around on the wedding day. Rent a party bus from the limo company instead. It often turns out to be much less expensive, and most bridal parties report that they love the atmosphere. Most party buses come equipped with great sound systems, mood lighting, comfortable chairs, and— perhaps most important after a long night of partying—a working restroom.

∼ The hotel your guests are staying at may provide free shuttle service. Most hotels have their own fleet of minibuses or vans to take their guests to and from airports and major shopping centers, so ask if you can schedule the bus to take your guests to the ceremony and reception and back afterward. If you've booked a significant block of rooms for your guests, or if you're holding your reception at that hotel's ballroom, the event manager will usually allow you to use the shuttle for free.

∽ The bridal party can drive themselves in a decorated minivan if one is available to them. Your parents', perhaps? Randi was able to arrange minivan transportation for her bridal party. Not only was it a "party bus," as she called it, but it didn't cost her a dime. The van was her parents'.

∽ After the reception, the bridal party may either be dropped off by a designated driver in his or her car, or if there will be no drinking, they can drive themselves home. A smart move would be to have the bridal party drop their cars off in the reception hall parking lot before the ceremony.

For the Guests

∽ There is usually no need for you to book transportation for your guests during the wedding weekend. Most guests either rent a car on their own, or they take taxis. Nearby relatives often offer to pick them up as well.

∼ Or, you can have the bridal party, friends, and relatives help transport out-of-town guests from the airport into town or to your house. No need to hire a shuttle or transport for them; this could cost you fifty to one hundred dollars depending on the number of guests coming in. You could pick them up yourself, but you might be too busy with final plans and fittings.

∼ If many guests will be coming into town from far away, they can use the hotel's shuttle bus, usually for free as part of a wedding room block.

23

Music for the Ceremony

The right music can add a lovely element to any wedding ceremony. This chapter shares ideas on how to hire musicians for less, get performances for free, and add a priceless personal touch to your day.

∼ First, check with the wedding officiant about your plans for music during the ceremony. You don't want to hire a harpist for $150 and then find out that the church does not allow out-side performers or the secular music you've selected. Another reason to talk to the officiant: he or she may have several wed-dings to perform that day—all within tight time constraints—and your music may put your ceremony time over the limit. Unfair, I know. But it does happen. It's best to ask first.

～ Have as one of your criteria for choosing a wedding site the free service of the location's musicians. See Chapter 12 for more details on the types of performers you might be able to book through your house of worship.

～ Remember, though, that the organist isn't always free. Tipping him or her is usually required.

～ If a relative, friend, or bridal party member is a professional musician, such as a harpist, pianist, or flutist, ask that person to perform at the ceremony as a wedding gift to you.

～ Place an ad in a college newspaper for a harpist or flutist to perform at your wedding. No doubt you'll soon be flooded with calls from talented young people searching for experience, résumé material, and a payment far below those expected by professional musicians. Anne paid just twenty-five dollars for the harpist who performed at her wedding. It was the young harpist's first job, and Anne loved her music. A professional she called while researching musicians claimed a two hundred dollar fee. Just be sure to first listen to the performer you hire.

～ Rather than hiring a soloist, why don't you sing a song to the groom yourself? Or have him sing to you. (This only works if you have a bit more singing experience than just performing "My Girl" on the karaoke machine.)

～ If your wedding will be held outdoors, have some of your wedding music played over a good stereo sound system. You can get a tape of classical or designated wedding music for free in the library, or borrow a CD from a recently married friend.

It was very hot on the day of my August wedding. Everyone was glad we weren't having songs performed during the ceremony, which allowed us to move inside more quickly after the ceremony was over in fifteen minutes.

—LYNN

～ If you'd like to hire a ceremony musician such as a pianist, you'll be surprised to find that most expert musicians don't charge an exorbitant price just to play ceremonies for an hour. Research musicians well, asking at local hotels for referrals to the pianists who play their brunches, and see if a one-hour package allows you the live music you want for less than you expected. David and Hannah were so happy with their pianist's rate that they hired him to play during the hour of the cock-tail party as well . . . for a grand total of one hundred dollars. "Hey, it wasn't Sting we were hiring!" says David.

24

The Photographer and Videographer

With the average photography package costing $2,000 and the average videography package costing $1,500, you're looking at a large expense for what is arguably a very important part of the day. You're paying for a permanent record of your wedding day, which adds up to a large amount for the finished products. Couples who try to save money often make a big mistake in underspending, and they pay the price later when they wind up with too few photos and a grainy wedding video. Learn how to find the happy middle ground of securing the best photos and footage for far less than average prices.

Average Spending for Photography and Video

	2008	2009	2010	2011	2012	2013
Photographer	$1,956	$2,017	$2,080	$2,144	$2,210	$2,279
Videographer	$1,546	$1,594	$1,643	$1,694	$1,747	$1,801

Printed with permission from TheWeddingReport.com.

The Photographer

~ When hiring a professional photographer, it's very important to comparison shop. Not only are you looking for the best prices and the best packages, you're also looking at the photographers' samples and the quality of their work. Are they dependable? Do they offer extras? Keep track of each photography service you consider so that you may narrow down the field later and choose from the best.

~ Ask a recently married friend to recommend her photographer. If she raves about his or her work and has attractive albums and portraits to support the glowing review, your search for quality has landed on a target. If the price is right, this photographer is a good choice.

∽ Note that membership in the Professional Photographer's Association of America means the photographer is well trained. It's a good way to check credentials.

∽ Hire a photographer who has at least five years of experience shooting weddings. A well-trained photographer can place all of your shots better, can assemble and capture group shots in less time than an amateur, and will get you better pictures than someone with little wedding experience. Hiring a true professional, especially given that expense, is the best investment.

∽ When looking through photographers' sample albums and photographs, look not only for focus and a pretty subject (they'll of course show you only their best work) but also for pictures taken in different lighting and different settings, a variation of vertical and horizontal shots, more candid than stiff posed shots, special lenses, and whatever other ideas you have for your album. You'll want to be sure you're getting every penny's worth when you hand over what could be a pretty hefty check.

∽ A quick check with the Better Business Bureau can reveal if any of your final choices for photographer have had any charges or complaints against them. You should know of your photographer's and videographer's past records if you're to trust them with such an important event.

Time Matters

◦ A less costly option would be to hire the photographer only for the ceremony and the beginning of your reception. After all, these are the most important times to capture. Plus, everyone looks their best the first half of the celebration. After a few hours guests look tired, makeup fades, and hairstyles fall. There would be no need to keep the photographer for the full five hours of the reception . . . particularly if your guests have cameras of their own. You can always get prints of their candid dancing scenes. One bride saved five hundred dollars with this option, and she noticed no huge difference in the quality of the photos from her reception.

◦ In your paying for the photographer's (and videographer's) time on your wedding day, every minute spent from the time of his arrival to his departure is on the clock. Keep that in mind when scheduling any break time between the ceremony and reception. Some brides schedule an hour or two-hour break before the reception starts, which is wasted money if the photographer is just standing around waiting for the next phase of the wedding to start.

Packages and Prices

~ Go through the photographers' lists of available packages. What is the minimum number of pictures you will need? Do you really need one thousand regular prints, twelve eight-by-tens, and one hundred wallets? You can save a lot of money by ordering just the number of pictures you'll need—to keep for yourself and to give as gifts. I've found that that an album of thirty photos, one eleven-by-fourteen, two eight-by-tens for parents, and one hundred wallets for thank-you notes is more than enough. When your print package gets to be too big, it can be overwhelming to choose and becomes a waste of money. Are you going to wallpaper a room with photos of your wedding? Most couples display two to five wedding photos in their home.

~ Most photographers will take only as many photos as specified in your package. So that might mean five hundred photos for a bargain package, one thousand photos for the next step up, and three thousand photos for the platinum package. Five hundred photos may be too few to allow for multiple shots of important moments all the way through the wedding and reception, so choose the next step up. It's worth it to have more choices rather than too few.

⌒ Don't be bullied by a set price package. See if you can pick and choose the elements you really want (you may not need wallet-sized photos) and negotiate the price accordingly. It's in the package that photographers rake in the cash, so assemble your package well.

⌒ If the photographer's package offers you the full set of proofs to keep for free, you're getting a nice stack of pictures that you would have had to pay for otherwise. Many bargain packages offer you two hundred free proofs, which is more than enough to keep. A three-hunded-proof package will allow you extra prints to make parents' albums with! For free!

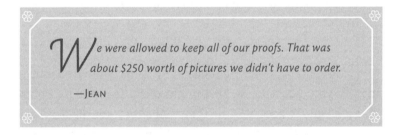

We were allowed to keep all of our proofs. That was about $250 worth of pictures we didn't have to order.

—JEAN

⌒ Ask if your proofs can be delivered on disk or online rather than as print photos, if you have to pay for the printing and delivery. Many photographers will be happy to avoid their own developing costs and just give you the online look instead of a proof sheet or prints.

✎ Ask what the photographer charges for prints ordered through a website. That's the real issue when it comes to your money. You don't want to be surprised by a twenty-five dollar charge for each five-by-seven. Photographers make most of their money from the prints their customers and their families order, so be sure you're aware of a pro's print prices as an important factor in whom you hire.

Albums

✎ Choose your album carefully. At the average photography studio it can cost more than $150 just for the album alone, without pictures! Choose a plain album, skipping the leather and decorated styles, as the real beauty will be inside the album. Don't pay to have your names printed on the album, as that's an extra cost as well.

✎ Ask about the price difference between one image per page and a scrapbook effect where five images are arranged on each page. If it costs the same, since it's all done digitally, you can get more photos in your album!

✎ Create a smaller formal bridal album. Go for a twenty-four- or thirty-six-page album rather than a forty-eight-page one. You'll still have your wedding pictures from the proofs you get to keep for free, plus the candids taken at the wedding by guests' cameras. The larger portrait-style photos in your main album are great for display, but you don't need many if you're on a budget.

~ Ask about inexpensive albums that offer slip-in photos in pockets that then seal. You'll avoid pricey professional album crafting, and you'll save 20 to 30 percent.

~ Another innovation in wedding albums is the new option of peel-and-stick album pages, where the photographer prints your portraits on special peel-and-stick paper and then applies the "sticker" right to the page. It looks amazing and costs 40 percent less.

~ If you don't want to decrease the number of pages in your album, you can certainly choose to have fewer shots in the parents' albums without them noticing the difference.

~ Don't be pressured into ordering special photo albums from the photographer for parents, grandparents, the bridal party, and others. For half the price of this service, you can make your own albums with extra copies of your pictures (perhaps some of the proofs or pictures taken with your camera) and inexpensive store-bought photo albums. You may even do your own wedding album using the professional pictures and a book you've purchased from the store. It all adds up to great savings if you do a good enough job arranging the pictures in the albums.

∼ Some brides choose to skip the professional bridal portrait, usually taken several weeks before the wedding.

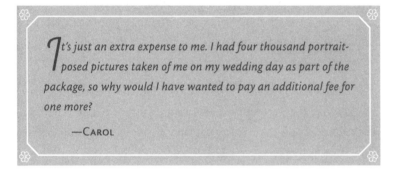

It's just an extra expense to me. I had four thousand portrait-posed pictures taken of me on my wedding day as part of the package, so why would I have wanted to pay an additional fee for one more?

—CAROL

∼ Skip the gimmick shots. Do you really need to pay extra for a picture of the two of you superimposed over the sheet music of "your song"? While it might be a fun memento, it's also a nonessential.

∼ Get a copy of the contract, just to clarify the specifics of your agreement and the package you've chosen, and keep your payment receipts in case any questions arise.

Volunteers

⁓ While many brides consider the wedding pictures too important to be left to an amateur, you may weigh your options differently. A friend or relative with plenty of photography experience can do just as wonderful a job as a pro, and he or she has the added advantage of knowing your guests and knowing what pictures you'll really want. Plus, you won't be charged anywhere near the fee of a professional photographer. Of course you'll pay for printing the pictures yourself.

⁓ Have two friends take pictures at the ceremony. Both could work the ceremony, providing different perspectives, and they could then take turns capturing special moments of the reception.

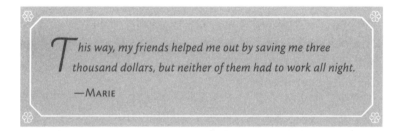

This way, my friends helped me out by saving me three thousand dollars, but neither of them had to work all night.

—MARIE

⁓ Have your volunteers use their own cameras so they don't have to learn the intricacies of someone else's during the ceremony. This is no time for trial and error. If, however, you have an outstanding camera and would prefer to use it for the wedding photos, give the camera to your volunteer a week or two before the wedding so he or she can get the hang of using it. Saving money usually means taking extra care to prevent the worst from happening.

> **Take Several Shots**
> *Tell your friend to take several shots of the major parts of the ceremony and reception so you won't lose all record of your first kiss if the one picture of it didn't come out. Several shots will be your insurance.*

One-Time-Use Cameras

⌒ Many brides are choosing to put throwaway cameras on each table at the reception. Guests then take candid shots of you, themselves, and all the dancing and fun going on around you. While you're dancing your first dance, Cousin Fred may be taking his cue to propose to his girlfriend . . . finally. Moments like these don't have to get away. Just make sure you don't overspend on the throwaway cameras. Each one will cost you anywhere from six to fifteen dollars, depending on where you shop—plus developing. If you figure the costs wisely, you can do this and still cut your wedding picture spending.

~ Look for brand-name one-time-use cameras, since the cheaper ones you may find online deliver poor-quality photos. Go to kodak.com for bargain-priced, wedding-decorated cameras.

~ Be careful of wedding cameras you find in the party supply store. They may be dirt cheap, but if they're nonbrand, you might sacrifice quality.

Developing

~ When comparison shopping for picture developing of one-time-use cameras and your own digital shots, consider that today's easy-to-use photo developing sites offer massive discounts. Kodak's online photo developing just ran a Memorial Day Weekend sale for ten-cent prints, down from their usual fifteen cents. Compare that to a photographer's per-photo charge of eight dollars!

Photo Printing Websites
Kodak Gallery—kodakgallery.com
Shutterfly—shutterfly.com
Snapfish—snapfish.com

These sites can also imprint gift items with your photos.

〜 Check out Costco's film developing charges, which are often far less than at a photo shop.

〜 Do not go to one of those one-hour developing places just because you can't wait to see your wedding photos. You'll just wind up paying three to five times extra for the convenience. Save some money and wait those few days.

〜 If you do have a favorite photo developing shop, ask if you can get a bulk discount for bringing in thirty one-time-use cameras or order a lot of prints off of your digital camera. Most shop owners will knock off 10 to 15 percent and throw in a few free five-by sevens! Customer loyalty is very important to them in this digital age, so you're in a good place to get a discount.

The Videographer

~ You may think that the wedding video is a rather unimportant part of the day. After all, you're going to be there, and it's the memories in your head that will last forever. While video pros warn against cutting expenses by eliminating the wedding video—or by asking a family member to take the footage—remember that your video is going to be more important to you ten years later than it is the week after your wedding. Not only is it a recording of your vows, your first dance, your cutting of the cake, it's a living memory of your loved ones. Over time, people age or pass away. In your video you'll have priceless footage of your uncle Augie laughing and singing with his brothers and sisters. You'll have footage of your father looking proudly at you. In the years to come, when these people are no longer in your life, you'll have this tape to remember them during the happiest times of their lives. I say often that it's a mistake to cut too deeply into your budget just to save money. The wedding video, for this reason, is worth some extra expense.

~ Comparison shop, again not only for price but for packages and quality. Look at the videographer's samples—the full-length ones, not the snippets of his or her best work. Look for focus, good lens work, graphics, smooth transitions, and soundtrack clarity.

⤳ Ask a friend to recommend her videographer; then take a look at her wedding video to see if it's the sort you would like. This is the best way to be sure you're getting your money's worth.

⤳ A true professional can do an in-camera edit, choosing shots well so that there is less need for heavy editing later on. Talk to your video pro about this practice. Cutting down on editing time will save you money later on.

⤳ Arrange for one camera shooting on your wedding day, instead of a two- or three-camera plan with extra workers hired to shoot your day from different angles. When you're on a budget, this pricey option isn't the best plan.

⤳ You can save several hundred dollars by forgoing the post-shooting edit. Videographer Steve Blahitka of Back East Productions in East Hanover, New Jersey, suggests buying the raw footage of your wedding for great savings. This is how it works: your professional videographer uses his experience to get the great shots, do in-camera edits, and then simply hands you the tape at the end of the night. No costly, by-the-hour editing fee means big savings, and you get to see your tape far sooner. Also, be aware that many videographers will edit your five-hour wedding day down to one hour of footage, so getting the raw tape will give you every minute of your day.

The Videographer's Style

Ask the videographer about his or her style. You don't want the video camera in your face all night, so make sure the videographer can get the footage without being underfoot. And ask what he or she wears to weddings. A suit? Tuxedo? Make sure this person will dress appropriately—this is your wedding.

～ Leave out special effects. This isn't Hollywood. It's your wedding video, and you don't need all the fancy editing work and effects that wind up dating your tape and distracting from the images. In addition, some effects are copyrighted, such as Disney characters, and cannot be used by the public.

～ Choose your video package carefully. How much time do you really think you'll need? Do you want to spend money on footage of you getting ready in the morning? Limit the number of hours the videographer will work and the number of locations, and you'll spend less.

～ How many copies do you really need? Prices vary wildly by videographer, so ask for a discount if you'll order more than three copies for yourself and your parents. Bridal party members don't need their own copies.

~ As with everything having to do with your planning, get a copy of your contract as a record of your agreement, complete with specific details and the videographer's signature or name. Keep all receipts as proof of payment.

~ While most experts agree that professional videography is the best investment, you may not have enough in your budget to warrant the use of a pro or may not have a large emotional investment in a top-notch video. In these cases, you can ask a reliable friend or relative to help out as a gift to you. Just realize that the quality will be lessened, as an amateur doesn't have the focus or devotion a professional would have.

~ Have two or three friends tape your wedding and reception with their video cameras from different angles. A good editing job will give your tape a professional look. With today's easy-to-use video editing software, you can create your own edited video, or you can have an experienced friend do this as his or her wedding gift to you.

Compare and Save

Professional videographer . . . . $1,500–$4,000

Friends helping out. . . . . free

∼ If your video volunteer will be using your video camera, give it to him or her a few days before the wedding to get used to it and its functions. Teach your friend how to use it. Point out fade-in, scanning, zooming, speed of movement, and so on. Then view together the practice filming.

∼ Skip the added expense of your videographer showing your baby photos. It's not needed.

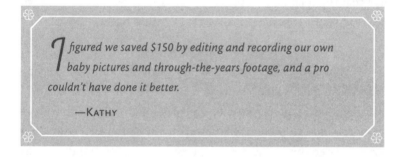

I figured we saved $150 by editing and recording our own baby pictures and through-the-years footage, and a pro couldn't have done it better.

—KATHY

∼ If you're planning to make copies of your self-shot wedding video for family and friends, buy DVDs for less at Staples or Office Max. You can't copy professional DVDs since they are copy-protected.

25

Wedding Programs and Printed Items

The program for your wedding day lets your guests know what to look forward to during your ceremony and who its participants are. Most important, the program remains one of your cherished keepsakes after the wedding. You can create beautiful programs for far less than standard commercial prices with the advice in this chapter.

~ Instead of ordering plain programs from the bridal stationery store or catalog—usually the same place you've ordered your invitations from—make your own. With a quality computer, your options are endless, and you have creative control over the process. Plus, today's paper companies are creating beautiful bridal-themed program paper at a cost of less than ten dollars for a pack of twenty-four. Some designs match the printer-ready styles of place cards and thank-you cards.

> **Compare and Save**
>
> 100 store-bought programs . . . . $75–$125
> 100 homemade programs . . . . $15–$40

~ Draw up your program, with precise wording and an idea of your layout. You'll need to know how many pages your program will be to figure copying costs. Of course, if you can fit your program on four sides (the fronts and backs of each side of a folded paper), you'll only need one sheet of paper for each program.

~ Visit mountaincow.com for inexpensive PrintingPress software that will allow you to design your own wedding programs, with easy-to-use templates for front cover and back cover text as well as inside text. This program offers a range of free graphics and fonts for the look of professional design without the big price tag.

~ If you like the look of calligraphy but don't trust your hand at it, use the calligraphy font on your home computer. You'll get flawless letters along with a neat page setup and (depending on your program) the ability to view the page on the screen without having to print it out first.

~ Save even more money by printing your programs on your computer. Use quality white or colored paper bought by the pound or in bulk at an office supply store or craft store, rather than spending more at an art supply store for designer papers. If your printer isn't top quality and your ink and paper are expensive, see if you can beat those costs by taking your master copy to a discount printer. Depending on the paper you choose, the total cost may be less, and the results will look great.

~ A decorative cover for your program is always a nice touch. Look in stationery stores, at religious bookstores, and on websites like pashweddings.com to find a good selection of program covers and comparison shop. They're not very expensive, but you want to get the best price you can.

~ Or, have an artist friend or relative design and create program covers for you. Again, it could be a gift, and it's a nice personal touch.

Compare and Save
Store-bought program covers . . . . $40–$75
Homemade program covers . . . . $10–$20

~ See if your printer will collate your programs and program covers and then bind them at the crease. Many places will do this for free. If not, simply fold each one and slip the program inside the cover unattached.

~ As nice as they are, programs may also be seen as nonessentials and cut from the wedding plans. You can live without them.

$\mathcal{P}$lace Cards

~ Don't spend a fortune on place cards from a bridal website or store. Your local craft and party supply stores have these on the cheap, often for 50 percent less, also preventing you from paying shipping costs.

~ Don't use computer-printed labels on your place cards. This is an etiquette don't and a waste of money. Handwrite the cards instead.

~ Get a second use out of your mountaincow.com PrintingPress software by loading its place card template and printing out your guests' names and table numbers with a great font.

enu Cards

~ Before you print out your own, ask if your reception site prints up menu cards for the guests' place settings or one per table. You don't want to waste paper and ink if your site does this for you.

~ Find attractive menu card stock at the craft store for far less than at bridal websites.

~ Use plain greeting card stock from the office supply store to create your own menu cards, at a cost of less than ten dollars. You don't need to attach your menu card stock to fabric-covered boards like you see at fine restaurants. Just the thicker card stock works very well and prevents added expense.

26

The Guest Book, Ring Pillows, and Other Items

Among the many items you'll cherish in years to come is your guest book. It's where your guests sign their names and leave you personal messages of good wishes and joy. With the ideas in this chapter you can supply a beautiful guest book without spending the high amounts in certain gift shops and catalogs. The same goes for your ring pillows and other keepsakes from the day.

✑ Don't buy one of those fancy, overpriced guest registry books in the bridal salon or in a bridal supply catalog. Instead, get a plain one at a discount stationery store. A white cover that says nothing is every bit as classy and appropriate as the kind with the shiny gold lettering and picture.

∼ You don't have to match your guest book to the design of your wedding invitations, as you'll see on some websites. Get a plain design instead. And avoid guest books that are dotted with crystals or other embellishments. That's just extra expense.

∼ Check your local craft store for guest books that can be decorated using glue-on ribbons and accent pieces. These often run less than fifteen dollars total.

∼ You'll also find guest books at the party supply store on the cheap, often no more than twelve dollars, a bargain compared to some forty-dollar guest books in celebrity collections.

∼ A wedding guest book is a great gift idea from the flower girl and ring bearer or other member of the wedding party.

∼ Forget the frilly feather pen that usually comes with those bridal guest book sets. A plain gold or white one you already own will do just as well.

∼ Make your own personalized guest book from a plain, unused journal found for less than five dollars at the bookstore.

~ Visit invitations4sale.com, the discount invitation website you have read about often in this book. They have guest books and unity candles that you can find in their 40-percent-off lists as well.

~ Appoint someone to be in charge of taking the guest book to the ceremony location, to the reception, and back home afterward. You don't want the book to be misplaced.

Ring Pillows

~ Comparison shop on bridal websites to see if you can catch these on sale for 15 percent off. Look during holiday sale times for great bargains.

~ Look in craft and party supply stores for an assortment of wedding accessories including simple and adorned ring pillows.

~ A crafty friend can make a ring pillow for you. It's an easy project and saves you more than fifteen dollars, particularly if you need two for two ring bearers.

*U*nity Candles

∿ Comparison shop at bridal websites for the best prices on a style you like.

∿ Check craft stores for unity candle kits, found for less than twenty dollars, that allow you to decorate your own pillar candle with a range of pins or other embellishments on the cheap.

∿ Buy a pillar candle and decorate it yourselves using separately purchased pearl-head pins, crystals, or other two-dollar crafting accents.

∿ Some couples don't want a unity candle. "You just have to blow it out, and then you have to store it someplace safe forever," says one bride from New York City. These couples consider their first kiss to be a sign of unity.

27

Decorating the Reception

You've seen advertisements and pictures of lavishly decorated ballrooms and banquet halls. Enormous floral centerpieces crown every table, ice sculptures highlight the buffet table, and billowing drapes of fabric with twinkling white lights hung from the ceiling transform the room into a magical scene. But what you don't see is the bill for such accoutrements. Decor is big business, and those lofty images demand a big investment. But you're not doomed to crepe-paper streamers and white balloons if your budget doesn't allow for the grand scenario. You can incorporate expensive looks for a lot less, choose equally impressive alternative decor ideas, and use your talents to design a million-dollar look for a fraction of the cost. Your guests won't be able to tell the difference.

〜 Use strings of white Christmas lights you already own to adorn trees or the ceiling in a dimly lit room. Or borrow white or colored Christmas lights from your family and friends to decorate a larger or outdoor setting for next to nothing. The smaller, nontwinkling lights provide the best effect.

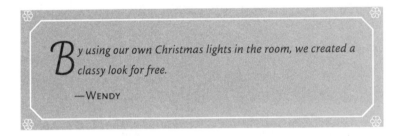

By using our own Christmas lights in the room, we created a classy look for free.

—WENDY

〜 Decorate the walls and buffet table with silver-framed pictures of you and your fiancé, your parents and siblings at their weddings, and your fiancé's relatives at their weddings. This is a favorite of many brides today. It's a touching tribute to special relatives, and it's virtually free.

〜 Decorate a ceiling or gazebo roof with mobiles you can make yourself. Choose from hearts, sparkles, crystals, stars, whatever you'd like. If you question the idea of mobiles, just hang straight lines with decorations at the ends. The result is your own starry sky. Check your local craft store for inexpensive materials.

~ Commission an artist or a culinary institute student to make an ice sculpture for you. Put an ad on the bulletin boards at a nearby school announcing your need for a sculptor. You may be able to have a sculpture made for around eighty dollars or even less, depending on its size and complexity. You can also ask your reception site manager if they would provide a free ice sculpture as part of their regular decor.

~ Ask your reception site manager what else they might provide as free decor. One site provides *chocolate* sculptures as part of their dessert buffet.

~ Rather than renting a trellis, use the one that's already in your yard or at the reception location.

~ For a theme wedding, use the items you have handy. For example, if you're planning a Mexican fiesta wedding, use your brother's souvenir sombrero as one of the decorations. Use your patterned rugs and throws as well. If you rented these items and others like them, you'd pay up to $150 easily.

~ If you don't own it, see if you can borrow it. If you can't borrow it, see if you can make it. If you can't make it, rent it.

~ At the very least, play up the natural attractions of the reception location. If there's a lovely view of the sunset, for example, part of the atmosphere is already set. Minimal decor is needed otherwise. So try to see your location at the time of day when your party will be taking place so you can get a look at the natural lighting and features.

28

Planning the Menu

Most often it's the food that guests remember. If the food is good, you'll hear raves. If it's not, you'll hear complaints. Many couples try too hard to save in this area of the expenses, but this is one place where you can't cut the budget too much. You get what you pay for. You can create a delicious, unique, and impressive menu by following the cost-saving tips in this chapter. Caterers and chefs alike tell me that they can answer to any budget challenge and still provide top-quality menu items that you and your guests will savor.

Initial Decisions

⌒ Before you can contract a caterer, you'll need to know exactly what kind of reception you'll be having—level of formality, theme, location, time of day. As mentioned previously, an earlier wedding may be a less formal one and may be less expensive if you will not be serving a full sit-down dinner. An afternoon wedding could mean a formal sit-down meal or just heavy hors d'oeuvres. An early evening wedding, before 8:00 P.M., usually includes a full dinner or buffet, and an after-eight reception is often served by hors d'oeuvres and cake. So obviously you'll need to know what kind of package and menu you're looking for before you can settle on a caterer.

Average Spending for Reception

According to theweddingreport.com, average spending for reception bar costs is around $2,000:

	2008	2009	2010	2011	2012	2013
Reception beverages/ bartender	$1,963	$2,023	$2,085	$2,148	$2,213	$2,280

Printed with permission from TheWeddingReport.com.

～ Do your research to compare the caterers available to you. Compare general costs, of course, along with other package elements such as equipment, linens, cleanup, and the like. Keep track of your notes and comparisons so that you can narrow the choices down when you're ready to make your final decision.

∼ Ask a recently married friend or relative to recommend the caterer who did her reception. If you remember the food at her reception as particularly outstanding and the service as exemplary, then you'll be able to make your choice based on experience. Several brides report savings of 10 to 15 percent as referrals from previous customers. Caterers depend on word-of-mouth advertisement, and you could save.

∼ When you're researching caterers, do the introductory work over the phone, but always go to the business in person for the next step. You'll want to see their samples, their linens and china if that's part of the package, and their overall appearance as a successful business. While there, arrange to taste their menu selections. Many caterers expect this request as part of today's smart wedding shopping, and they keep a supply of hors d'oeuvres on hand.

∼ A good standard by which to measure possible caterers is their membership in the National Association of Catering Executives (nace.net). Membership in this organization listed on the company's business card means the caterer is well trained and has met the requirements of the association.

 The Better Business Bureau can tell you if any charges or complaints have been registered against the caterers you're researching. A good history in the business is a positive indication of their reliability, whereas a negative mark could make you think twice about investing in that business's services. After all, it's your wedding.

Choosing a Caterer

Use your best instincts when researching caterers. Are they forthcoming with information? Do they seem willing to go by your wishes, or do they seem to want to be in control? Do they seem organized? Do you feel comfortable with them?

Food Choices

When you've settled on a caterer, choose your menu carefully. The courses and foods you choose will undoubtedly affect the price you're paying, so follow these hints from brides who have been there.

 Choose a menu that is right for the season of your wedding. Some heavier foods should not be served in the summer.

∼ Ask for a price list for each type of entrée or appetizer. Your caterer should be able to provide you with this information so you can tell at a glance which choices are less expensive.

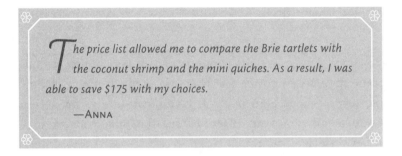

> *The price list allowed me to compare the Brie tartlets with the coconut shrimp and the mini quiches. As a result, I was able to save $175 with my choices.*
>
> —ANNA

∼ Choose more popular, simpler foods. Exotic choices mean more money. Chef Jerome Louie of the Bernards Inn in Bernardsville, New Jersey, suggests asking your caterer about his or her creative choices in chicken and pasta dishes. Chicken and pasta are less expensive than meat dishes, and they can be prepared in unexpected gourmet ways, making them seem more exotic and more expensive.

∼ Choose a less expensive option of a pricey dish. For instance, choose medallions of beef or beef tenderloin rather than filet mignon. A great chef can prepare these options with flair and taste, plus great presentation, and your guests will never know that you saved ten dollars per plate with this choice.

~ Choose less expensive meats. Chicken, turkey, and pork are much less expensive than filet mignon and can be prepared with gourmet flair.

~ Look into prices for combination dinners. Chef Jerome Louie suggests an entrée featuring two grilled jumbo shrimp and several medallions of beef. Combination plates can cost less, depending on your selections, and they give your guests a better variety of food.

~ Try something beyond the usual bridal menu fare. For instance, instead of filet mignon, chicken marsala, and salmon, consider Australian rack of lamb. Unique choices may be priced lower.

~ Choose in-season foods to save money. Select seafoods that are in season. Your chef can let you know a week before the wedding what the prices of tilapia, salmon, and sea bass are doing on the market. You'll then choose the best-priced options. The same goes for fruits and vegetables.

∼ Comparison shop for seafood. In many cases, calamari and mussels are half the price of shrimp cocktail. Ask your caterer to show you the high-to-low pricing on his or her seafood dish price sheet.

∼ Check the market price of meats. Various meats are pricier in certain seasons, so allow your chef to make choices on meat dishes closer to the wedding date to take advantage of better pricing. Pork might be a better buy than chicken, so perhaps a station can be built around that ingredient. It does add up.

∼ Choose unique pastas for the cocktail party stations, for a course, or for an entrée. Spinach and goat cheese ravioli or pumpkin manicotti are gourmet treats your guests will think you spent a lot of money to serve them. Pastas can also be served with seafood garnish for an extra-tasty touch.

∼ Select more inexpensive food stations for the cocktail hour. There is no need for a carved meat station during the pre-party when you're paying for a meat entrée during the dinner. You'll save hundreds of dollars by "cutting out" the carved prime rib, ham, pork loin, or lamb chops.

∼ Have fewer food stations during the cocktail hour to save a few hundred dollars off your bill. Do you really need twelve food stations? Guests would be happy with half, provided the food at each is high quality.

～ One station that is surprisingly inexpensive is the fajita station, since each dish is about one-quarter meat and the rest vegetables and tortillas. Add toppings, and guests are often thrilled to get "the real deal" that's way better than what they prepare at home.

～ Also inexpensive is the Asian station, since this too is often only one-quarter meat or seafood. Chefs say the addition of big bowls of egg noodles, basmati rice, Jasmine rice, and condiments looks expensive but really costs 20 percent less than other stations.

～ Fill your buffet with colorful, lush green salads including mesclun, spring greens, endive, and other leafy splendor, topped with fresh or grilled vegetables, for a gourmet spread on the cheap.

～ Chef Shai Tertner of Shiraz in New York City suggests that you have these dramatic salads served in colorful bowls or giant woks for added visual punch. *Any* foods served in brightly colored bowls or on ice platters always look more amazing to guests. So ask the catering manager about square platters, bright red cocktail plates, and other designs outside of traditional white dishes. They will often let you use their other sets for free, just for the asking.

~ By virtue of choosing foods your guests don't get at every other wedding, it will seem like you spent more. So allow your chef to get creative with chicken skewers, tapas, vegetable rolls, and other treats.

~ Skip a course. Guests don't need a salad if you had a salad during the cocktail hour. Or combine the salad course with the appetizer course, such as serving a crab cake with a mesclun salad on one plate so that you can serve a slightly smaller crab cake, or just one rather than two.

~ In colder weather, serve soup. It's a crowd-pleaser, and it usually costs a lot less per person depending on which type of soup you choose. A lobster bisque will cost more than a tomato bisque.

~ Sushi stations are among the more expensive options at cocktail parties. Guests can have sushi any day of the week. Replace this with a less expensive grilled vegetable station.

∼ Don't just have the cheap stations like a pasta bar and a mashed potato bar. Guests will sense that you "cheaped out," and they'll be less than pleased with an all-carb menu. Add in some great meat stations to give you a variety.

∼ One popular, inexpensive station is the pierogi bar. These potato-stuffed ravioli can be topped with an array of sauces or toppings such as sour cream, horseradish sauce, mushroom sauce, cheddar cheese, goat cheese, and mustards.

∼ Skip the big cheese-cube tray during the cocktail hour. It will hardly be touched if you're offering other selections, and it can go bad if left out too long.

∼ Don't plan on having a seafood bar or other specialty food bar set up at the reception if other food will be served. While the choice may be appetizing, it's an expensive nonessential.

∼ Follow the big trend toward comfort foods, such as little glasses of macaroni and cheese, grilled cheese sandwiches, mini cheeseburgers, and gourmet flavored french fries, which all cost 20 percent less than other traditional cocktail party fare.

∼ Avoid obviously expensive foods such as caviar, filet mignon, and lobster tails.

~ For the entrée, have the caterer offer your guests a choice of a meat or nonmeat entrée. Not only will this lower the price quoted in your contract, you'll please your health-conscious guests.

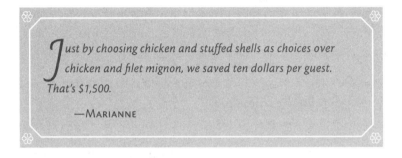

Just by choosing chicken and stuffed shells as choices over chicken and filet mignon, we saved ten dollars per guest. That's $1,500.

—MARIANNE

~ Dress up an inexpensive chicken or pasta dish with a great sauce. Chefs can work wonders with a seafood sauce or an amazing mushroom sauce, again making it seem more gourmet.

~ Use seafood as a garnish. Rather than offering king crab legs, for instance, serve a bit of crabmeat on top of a pasta dish.

~ Serve meals family style, with big platters set in the center of each guest table, for a help-yourself serving mode that can cost 10 to 15 percent less.

〜 Do you really need several different kinds of vegetables? Cut down the list and save some money. Everyone's going to be saving room for the cake anyway.

〜 Ask for creative presentations of vegetables, such as serving several asparagus spears tied with a length of chive, mashed potatoes piped onto the plate in a swirl, and other fun touches.

〜 Check out flavored risottos as a great side dish that pleases guests and doesn't cost a lot.

〜 The manner in which the food is served may also affect the caterer's final bill. Rather than set out a big tray of shrimp cocktail or other appetizers, caterers strongly recommend having these items passed by servers. This way each guest's portion is controlled and the caterer's fees for these menu choices are lowered. Caterers say guests consume 20 percent less when hors d'oeuvres are hand passed. That savings comes back to you.

〜 Or arrange a more economical deal with your caterer. Have the caterer prepare the food, and you do the rest. You pick it up, set it up, and clean it up. This can save you up to 30 percent off your bill. Or along the same lines, contract for only half of the meal to be catered. The caterer does the entrée, and you do the appetizers and desserts.

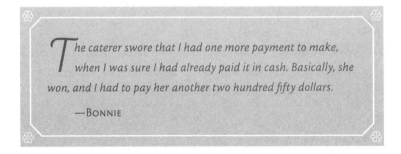 Don't go for expensive food decorations and displays. You don't need a shrimp cocktail sculpture in the shape of a three-dimensional heart, do you? Believe it or not, you could wind up paying up to three hundred dollars for a food sculpture such as this.

~ Get a copy of the contract, including a full, in-detail listing of the package and menu you're purchasing. As an added precaution, get the name of the person who took your order, and write down the date and time it was taken. Keep all payment receipts and perhaps even a copy of your check, in case of conflict over the bill later on.

> *The caterer swore that I had one more payment to make, when I was sure I had already paid it in cash. Basically, she won, and I had to pay her another two hundred fifty dollars.*
>
> —BONNIE

Self-Catering

If you'll be catering the reception yourself, consider the following tips.

~ Arrange for some members of your bridal party and perhaps some relatives and friends to help out in the kitchen a few days before the wedding.

~ If you'll self-cater part of your reception, go to Costco for economical party platters, frozen hors d'oeuvres, and seafood.

~ Plan to buy trays of specialty food from your local deli or the takeout section at the caterer's. Just transfer the Swedish meatballs and bacon-wrapped Brie onto serving plates, and you have catered quality for a near homemade price.

~ Use the menus you've found in the caterers' brochures to plan your appetizers and entrées. You'll find you can plan and serve identical meals for a fraction of caterers' prices.

~ Plan your own menu around popular, inexpensive foods such as pasta, chicken, and in-season seafood.

~ Use your favorite recipes. This is no time to try new ones.

⌁ If you'd like to serve some ethnic foods at your reception, check with your local heritage organization. They may be able to help you with recipes, pricing, and even their own frozen selections. One bride received a big 30 percent discount and some help in the kitchen from her heritage association's expert cooks.

⌁ Borrow the extra equipment you'll need, such as baking pans, stockpots, and so on. No need to rent them.

⌁ Shop in bulk. Check wholesale markets for the ingredients you'll need.

⌁ When pricing food and supplies, always shop by unit prices. You can always discover hidden bargains that way.

⌁ Garnish plates of your appetizers to give them a professional look. Your guests will never know.

⌁ Decorate the appetizer table with flowers and framed pictures so that the full table makes it look like there's more food.

⌁ Volunteer helpers can set up, serve, and clean up. Good people to ask are friends of your younger brother (he'll have a better time if they're there) and your friends' children.

29

Beverages

There will be many toasts and trips to the bar for your guests, so you'll want to find the most economical way to supply drinks. Don't cut expenses too deeply here, as you won't want your guests to toast you with something you wouldn't drink on a bet. Forget about a cash bar; that's an insult and a major no-no in the wedding world today. Here you'll learn how to arrange top-notch beverages for your guests at a bargain, without the savings showing.

～ For most brides, the idea of an open bar goes without saying. Their families would expect no less, and they'd consider a cash bar to be an attack on their station in life. So instead of canceling the open bar and risking the wrath of your relatives, choose instead to limit the choices offered at that open bar. Have the bartender offer a smaller range of wines, mixed drinks, and soft drinks instead of opening the place's full stock to your guests.

~ For information on today's best wines and spirits, plus a reliable price list, check out the highly esteemed Wine Spectator at winespectator.com. Here you'll be able to compare wine information, descriptions of taste, and, most important, expense. Be sure to visit your local upscale liquor store to purchase several different bottles a few months beforehand. Invite some friends over for a wine tasting, and make your choices on reds and whites for your reception. Two months or so before your wedding, consult with the liquor store manager for a discount on several cases of the chosen vintages.

~ Check first to see if your location has any liquor restrictions. If you find out too late that it doesn't have a liquor license, you won't be able to use your supplies. That's hundreds of dollars wasted.

~ Eliminate pricier drinks like Long Island iced teas that have a lot of liquor in them.

~ Serve mid-priced drinks that will keep your guests happy for less. Arrange for a margarita bar, perhaps served outdoors for a great treat at a mid-level price tag. Or, serve beautiful pitchers of sangria.

✎ Serve mid-shelf liquors instead of pricier top-shelf liquors.

✎ Don't allow shots at your bar. The pure alcohol consumption raises your bar tab.

✎ Supply your own wines and hard liquors purchased at a discount liquor store, if your site allows you to bring in your own beverages.

✎ Ask if the site has "dead stock," which is the supply of wines that they've just removed from their wine list to make room for a new vintage, and you may get those cases in their basement (which are perfectly fine) for half the price.

✎ Skip the champagne toast. Guests can toast you with the drinks they already have in their hands. Plus, not everyone likes champagne. Or arrange to provide only one glass of champagne per guest—just for the toast. You'll limit your needs to only eight or ten bottles of champagne, rather than twenty or thirty.

✎ For an afternoon wedding, provide fabulous champagne punches in mango, berry, and lime flavors. They're bright and colorful with fresh fruit slices in them, and guests love the novelty of a liquored-up punch.

〜 Choose to serve nonalcoholic drinks only at an afternoon wedding. Fruit punches and iced teas are the perfect quenchers for a tenth of the price of liquor.

〜 Close the bar early. Not only will you save money, but your guests will have more time to dance off their champagne before having to leave.

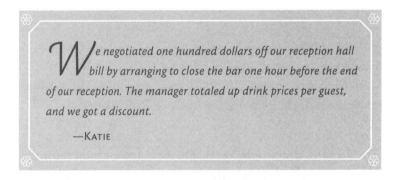

We negotiated one hundred dollars off our reception hall bill by arranging to close the bar one hour before the end of our reception. The manager totaled up drink prices per guest, and we got a discount.

—KATIE

〜 Be aware of whether the establishment charges a corkage fee, an extra expense when you supply the liquor. It's a big waste of money if you're paying ten dollars each time the bartender opens a bottle of your wine. Negotiate that charge out of your contract.

〜 Appoint someone to ask the bartenders to stop opening bottles of wine an hour before the end of the reception. You have to pay for every bottle opened, so if there are already five bottles uncorked and half-consumed, have bartenders pour from those instead.

∼ If your wedding will take place in a hotel, ask if you can have the unfinished wine bottles sent up to your suite for an after-party, or sent to your bridal party's rooms for a post-wedding party.

✑*oft Drinks*

∼ Arrange for a great array of soft drinks, including root beer, cream soda, orange soda, and black cherry soda in addition to the usual Coke and Sprite.

∼ Provide flavored iced teas, including peach, mango, white tea, blackberry, and other flavors.

∼ Garnishes add special touches to soft drinks, so ask about fruit spears and other garnish tricks you can have for free.

∼ Especially at outdoor weddings, guests love their ice-cold water. So make sure each table has fresh pitchers. And guests will usually drink less at the bar when they have access to refreshing water with lemon slices—for free.

After-Dinner Drinks

〜 Forget the liquored coffee drinks like Irish and Jamaican coffee. Regular coffee works fine at the end of a great wedding.

〜 Ask if your site manager will give you the international coffee bar for free. Many sites want to make you happy so you'll refer them to others, and they're happy to throw in this inexpensive perk.

〜 Guests can order brandy and cognac for themselves back at their hotel bar. Eliminate these pricey liquor drinks from your reception and save hundreds of dollars.

〜 Ask if dessert martinis are possible on your budget, or perhaps as an add-on to your reception package. Chocolate martinis are a great treat for guests, and you might choose to serve these instead of an international coffee bar.

〜 For a fun twist on after-dinner drinks for a fall or winter wedding, serve gourmet hot chocolate at the dessert bar. Add chocolate shavings, fresh whipped cream, and marshmallows for the full effect.

30

The Cake

The star of the wedding menu is always the cake. Celebrities spend tens of thousands on theirs, knowing that the cake will wind up on a television special or the cover of a magazine. Your cake can be just as beautiful but at a far lower price. Here you'll find out how to select the perfect confection without getting iced on the price.

Average Spending for Cake

	2008	2009	2010	2011	2012	2013
Cake	$544	$562	$580	$599	$618	$638
Cake knife set	$44	$45	$46	$47	$49	$51
Cake topper	$42	$43	$44	$45	$46	$47

Printed with permission from TheWeddingReport.com.

Where to Find the Cake

~ Don't order your cake through a bridal salon. Some offer such services in their bridal packages, but you could wind up paying five hundred dollars for a simple three-tier cake.

~ You'll get a better price if you order your cake from a baker rather than a caterer. Only your comparison shopping can tell you for sure what the specifics are, of course, but this is a general prescript.

~ Use your family's regular bakery. You know they're reliable, you've tasted their cakes before, and you just might get a discount for being a regular customer. One bride recently received a 50 percent discount from her family's regular bakery.

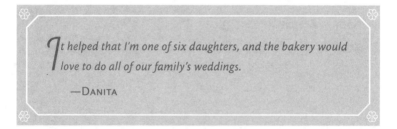

It helped that I'm one of six daughters, and the bakery would love to do all of our family's weddings.

—DANITA

∾ Comparison shop at bakeries of different sizes, in different parts of town. Their prices will definitely vary, and you won't always get a better cake in a larger bakery.

∾ When comparison shopping at bakeries you've never been to before, always ask to sample a piece of their wedding cakes. It's not as strange a request as it sounds, and it's the best way to be sure you're getting a good cake for your money.

∾ Ask a recently married friend where she ordered her wedding cake, and get yours at the same place if the price is right.

∾ If you'll be attending a wedding in the near future, ask the bride where she ordered her cake. You may find out about a great source with low prices.

∾ For an informal wedding with no three-tiered bridal cake, see if your supermarket bakery's sheet cakes are pretty enough for you . . . at one-third the price of a traditional wedding cake!

∾ For the same style of informal cake, check Costco's bakery department for steep discounts.

∾ Does the bakery deliver the cake to the reception location for free, or is there a charge? Ask before you order.

$\mathcal{O}$*rdering the Cake*

~ When ordering your wedding cake, you'll have to tell the baker how many guests will be in attendance at your wedding. Take ten off your grand total since not everyone eats cake at the reception. There are those who skip the cake because they're dieting, on special medical orders not to have sweets, or too busy dancing to sit down for a slice of cake. The smaller number means you'll be paying that much less for your bakery-made cake. Just don't go too low—you wouldn't want to have guests left without a piece.

~ At some bakeries, stacked cake layers are less expensive than wedding cake layers that are set up in tiers, separated by decorative columns or swan figurines. Ask your baker about the price difference for a cake with layers stacked instead of supported.

~ Ask for a copy of the order for your cake, checking twice to make sure the baker has recorded the right size, filling, icing, decorations, time and date of wedding, location of the reception, and phone number to reach you. A lost or wrong cake is one of the most common wedding blunders, and it's also a waste of your money.

∽ Call to confirm the delivery and order of your cake once or twice during the planning months and then once again several days before the wedding.

Elements of the Cake

∽ Choose a smaller cake, perhaps just three tiers instead of five. That's usually more than enough to feed over one hundred guests.

∽ To cut down on the expense of a baker making and decorating a big cake, order a two-tiered decorated cake for display and the cutting ceremony, and then have the reception hall serve your guests from that cake as well as a plain sheet cake with the same filling and frosting that they have kept in the kitchen. No one will be able to tell. Your savings are 20 to 30 percent.

∽ Forget about the trend of having a separate mini wedding cake at each guest table. That adds up to a lot of labor, extra frosting and toppings, and a higher price tag.

∽ Make sure you choose fillings and frosting that will do well in the weather. A hot summer day could cause your cake to melt right off the table. It has happened. A buttercream frosting usually holds up better than a frosting made of whipped cream. Keep the cake in the shade and as cool as possible on warm days.

~ Ask for a price list of fillings and cake flavors. Most bakeries and bakers offer their standard flavors of white cake, vanilla cake, chocolate cake, and the like with several different kinds of buttercream and fruit fillings, with their "gourmet" flavors of carrot cake and cannoli fillings costing a few dollars more per slice. That adds up to several hundred dollars extra. Stick with the standards and save.

~ See if you can save by going smaller *and* gourmet. One couple chose a smaller wedding cake so that their guests could feast on rich chocolate cake with cannoli cream filling. The price shift was worth it, as their guests raved about it being the best wedding cake they'd ever had. How's that for a sweet reward?

~ While the smooth, sculpted look of rolled fondant makes for a great picture and bridal magazine cover shot, it's also far more expensive than traditional frosting with buttercream icing. At several weddings I've been to there were complaints that although the cake was a work of art, the stiff fondant outer layer was inedible.

∼ Skip the rum-based filling and other liquor-infused cakes. They can cost up to five dollars more per slice!

∼ Even in the cake industry, time is money. While choosing your cake style and decorations, remember that the intricate design piped in icing on the sides of your cake layers could take hours for a bakery artist to complete. You will pay dearly for it. Yes, it is a beautiful sight when the baker presents a cake that looks like it's covered in lovely Belgian lace, but you'd pay far less for a traditionally frosted cake with piped-on accents or a cascade of fresh flowers. The same price increase applies to marzipan minisculptures. The more artistry it takes, the more time it takes, and the more it will cost.

The Groom's Cake

∼ Make the groom's cake yourself, or have a relative or friend make the groom's cake.

∼ Look in your supermarket bakery or Costco for great, inexpensive cakes that would fill this tradition at a big discount.

∼ Skip the groom's cake altogether, especially if you're having a small or informal wedding.

Additional Desserts and Coffee

~ Forget the extra dessert trays and the chocolate mousse. Let them eat cake. Savings here could reach thirty dollars per guest.

~ Skip the international coffee bar. Order plain and decaffeinated coffee instead. Coffees can be served with flavored syrups to give guests a taste they don't get all the time.

~ Skip the Viennese table of endless desserts. Guests don't need that many choices, and especially after a big meal most of it goes to waste.

~ Have wedding cake plus one exotic additional dessert, such as a mango sorbet or a chocolate mousse cake. Have just wedding cake and chocolate-dipped strawberries for a savings of more than fifteen dollars per guest.

~ Skip the bananas flambé. That and other cooked desserts are just a waste of money.

~ As your cake-plus-one-dessert option, set out a refreshing platter of fresh fruit that's in season and cut masterfully for a great design. Include pineapple, bing cherries, papaya, and other unique fruits that aren't at peak price.

∼ Skip the chocolate fountain. With rental of the machine and all of those dipping items, the price adds up . . . and guests have seen this hundreds of times. It's not worth the extra charge to have it at your reception.

∼ Bring in the taste of childhood for an inexpensive dessert station such as an ice cream, gelato, or sorbet bar. Or try a big new trend on the cheap: the pudding bar, including chocolate, vanilla, pistachio, and lots of fresh whipped cream and candy toppings, served in martini glasses.

∼ Cupcakes are still a top choice on a budget, with a color-coordinated icing plan and two different flavors for guests to choose from.

∼ A real crowd-pleaser on a budget is the cookie station, with lots of different types of cookies served on silver platters.

∼ Also hot on the cheap: a crepe station with cherry or apple filling and fresh whipped cream.

∾ Just have petit fours on individual platters set on each guest table at dessert time. This can cost as little as three dollars per guest and is great for your cake-plus-one-dessert option.

∾ For at-home or informal weddings where you can bring in your own food, get a bulk box of ice-cream sandwiches from Costco. Guests will love the ice-cold treats and the familiar taste of childhood. A box of these can cost less than twenty-five dollars to feed forty or so guests.

∾ For informal or at-home weddings, ask relatives and friends to make their favorite desserts and bring them along as their wedding gift to you.

On Top of the Cake

You could buy traditional cake-top decorations at the bakery, or you could put something else on the cake.

∾ Top off your cake with a special item or gift. A crystal heart figurine is a gorgeous topper, but make sure the baker knows exactly how much it weighs and its size so the precious thing doesn't fall off the cake onto the floor. The same goes for anything else you're planning to top your cake with. Those expensive crystal toppers with doves and butterflies may be too fragile to place on the cake, and if the topper snaps, the entire cake may be inedible because of shards of lead crystal or glass!

~ Decorate your cake with flowers. Just wash them well, let them air dry, and make sure they're not poisonous. Check with your baker as to which flowers usually go on cakes as decorations; then check with your florist about the safety of those flowers. Saving money should never be a health hazard.

~ Top your cake with an item you own, such as a little alumni flag or a toy, or borrow a cake topper from your parents, grandparents, siblings, or in-laws to keep the tradition in the family.

~ Check floral wholesalers or your craft store for inexpensive decor on a wire, such as butterflies or colorful circles, and have the cake baker place these around the cake for accenting.

Compare and Save

Cake decor from a bridal website............. $30

Craft store accents with wire $12

⌒ Or see if you can negotiate the cake top for free as part of the cake package.

The Cake Cutter

⌒ Don't choose from those offered in bridal salons or bridal catalogs unless you find them on sale.

⌒ Don't get a cake cutter set engraved with your names and wedding date. That can cost anywhere from thirty to more than one hundred dollars depending on the wording you want engraved.

⌒ Have a friend or relative give the cake cutter to you as a wedding gift. You might even receive a pretty engraved one.

⌒ Visit invitations4sale.com for up to 40 percent off cake knife sets.

⌒ Borrow your parents', grandparents', or in-laws' cake knife set for free.

〜 If you're not one to treasure your wedding cake cutter forever, just use the reception hall's serving knife.

〜 See if your bakery offers a wedding cake cutter set as part of the wedding cake package. Some companies add this in as a free perk!

〜 Buy a neat dessert knife at a home decor store such as Bed Bath & Beyond, and decorate it yourself using a length of ribbon, or leave it undecorated because the silver handle is so attractive. The cost? Less than ten dollars.

31

Reception Entertainment

DJ or band? Strolling violinist or a twelve-piece orchestra? Swing danc-
ing or the chicken dance? The entertainers you select will make or break
your wedding celebration, so get the most for your money without sacri-
ficing fun and photo opportunities on your big day. The entertainment
industry has changed a lot in the past few years, offering new combina-
tions and packages that can help you wow your guests and give everyone
a night to remember. Check out this chapter for some smart cost-cutting
measures and avoid the deadliest mistake of all: hiring cheap talent.

Deciding on Style and Possibilities

~ Consider the type of music you want. The performer you
choose should have a broad repertoire, whether classical or pop.

A band's inability to play the kind of music you like narrows the field of possibilities by one.

Average Spending for Ceremony and Reception Entertainment

	2008	2009	2010	2011	2012	2013
Band	$1,786	$1,842	$1,900	$1,960	$2,022	$2,085
DJ	$702	$724	$747	$770	$794	$819
Musicians	$493	$508	$524	$540	$557	$574

Printed with permission from TheWeddingReport.com.

~ Compare packages. What can each DJ or band offer you? When you compare specifics, you'll get a better idea of what your money will be getting you. For instance, one group's bargain price may be for five hours of playing while the other's is for four hours. Do the math.

~ A major factor in choosing the entertainment is the amount of space you'll have available for them. A band works well in a spacious reception hall with a stage, but a wedding at home or in a smaller room creates limitations on your choice. A DJ or soloist is perhaps the better selection for these smaller locales. Don't book too big a group for the space you have available.

~ Consider the facilities of your reception location. Level ground is needed for DJs and most bands, and it's best to make sure your location has enough electrical outlets and power. An unforeseen problem means you could lose your entertainment at the last minute, along with the nine hundred dollars you paid for it.

~ Consider your crowd when searching for a DJ or band. If your guests are older, you'll want to provide music they'll appreciate. The same goes for your younger guests. So arrange music according to what your guests will actually dance to. The type of music will determine the kind of band or DJ you'll get.

~ If you're having trouble deciding between a DJ and band, treat them as equals when you do your comparison shopping and just go for the better prices and packages.

$\mathcal{D}$J or Band

∼ A DJ is usually less expensive than a band because there are fewer people working and fewer people to feed at the reception. Compare price packages, because some DJs consider themselves "upscale" and have astronomical packages.

Mix-and-Match Entertainment
According to Dennis Tessler at The Pros (prosentertainment .com), you can choose from tiers of entertainment services. On the average, a DJ will cost eight hundred to two thousand dollars for the night. A live band will run three thousand to five thousand dollars. With the mix-and-match system, you can hire one or two DJs and a live singer for three songs and get an upgraded sound system for one thousand to fifteen hundred dollars combined. That's getting the best of both worlds for a comparable price. Other options you might find in these new entertainment packages include lighting upgrades and light shows, multiple singers, professional dancers, and party props.

∼ Get both. A new trend in the wedding entertainment industry is the merging of DJ and band options. You'll see entertainment packages in which you can provide a DJ at your reception, plus a few live performances by a singer or musician. Entertainment professionals are always taking the pulse of what's wanted by brides and grooms, and the rising popularity of this mix-and-match entertainment lineup means that you can practice your negotiating skills once again to book both live and recorded music for your day.

∾ Not all entertainment companies have caught the wave of the future, and you may find yourself staring at a contract that *includes* light shows and party props. If these elements are not to your liking, ask to have them removed from the package and the price differential revealed. Remember, wedding professionals are competing among themselves for your business and referrals. You have great negotiating power; use it to get the best service for the best price in this expensive portion of the wedding budget.

∾ Find out what the fees are for adding extra hours at the end of the evening. Your whole group may be having so much fun at the reception that you decide to ask the DJ or band to stay on for one more hour. What are the extra charges for doing so, or is it just another hourly rate? It's important to know this ahead of time, as a decision made at the actual reception could cost you a small fortune in additional fees.

∽ Compare prices per hour versus flat fees, and figure out how many hours you think your reception will last. Ask your recently married friend how long her reception went on and whether or not she wanted to add on a few more hours at the end of it.

∽ Get recommendations from recently married friends, or hire a group you've already seen at another wedding.

∽ Better yet, if you're going to hire a band, go hear them at an actual reception if you can. No one will mind if you step in to listen for a moment.

DJ Attire

If you're checking out a DJ, find out what he or she will be wearing to the reception. State your preference for a suit or tuxedo for a man, or a dress or tuxedo for a woman.

∽ Specify how many breaks the band will be allowed to take during the reception. You don't want to pay them for five hours of playing when they've really only played for three.

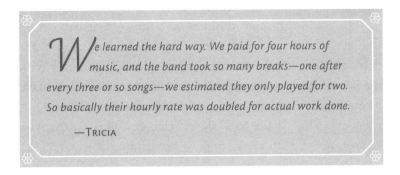

We learned the hard way. We paid for four hours of music, and the band took so many breaks—one after every three or so songs—we estimated they only played for two. So basically their hourly rate was doubled for actual work done.

—TRICIA

∼ Draw up a contract and get signatures for verification. Record the date and time of the contract as well.

∼ As an added precaution—and this comes from a bride who learned a lesson the hard way—specify the kind of music the band will be playing and all of the band members' names.

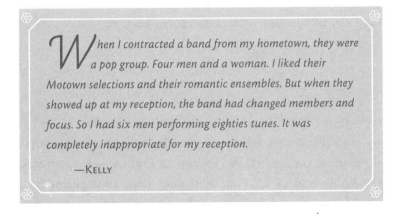

When I contracted a band from my hometown, they were a pop group. Four men and a woman. I liked their Motown selections and their romantic ensembles. But when they showed up at my reception, the band had changed members and focus. So I had six men performing eighties tunes. It was completely inappropriate for my reception.

—KELLY

~ To avoid the same problem, recognize that bands may change lead singers and selections during the six months between the contract and the wedding. Keep in contact with the band—just tell them you're confirming again—and make sure your contract lets you out of the agreement without monetary obligation if the band should change. (This, by the way, is a reason why DJs are so popular at weddings.)

~ Give the DJ or band you're hiring a list of songs you'd like to hear at your reception, including special numbers such as line dances and group numbers. Also give them a list of songs you don't want them to play. Some songs may remind you of other times, other places, and other people, and you want to make sure they're not a part of your day.

~ Get a copy of your payment receipt and a copy of your check as proof of payment. Money questions later down the road can be silenced with good record keeping.

No Pros?

~ If a friend or a family member has a band or is a professional musician, let him or her play for a while, perhaps during the band's breaks. Of course, if your talented acquaintances would like the exposure of working your entire reception—

and they sound good to you—arrange an amount you could pay them. If they refuse payment, offer them a free meal instead, or simply accept their performance as a gift. One bride arranged for her stepbrother's band to play at her wedding as his gift to her. The savings: $650 she would have had to pay to a professional group.

∾ Hire a college or high school musical group to perform at your reception. These young people studying to be professional musicians or instructors take their performances seriously, and you'll only have to pay them a fraction of what you'd pay a professional.

∾ Or ask the person who performed at your ceremony to play a few hours at the reception as well. Using one person for both saves you time and money.

∾ Have a friend of the family or a colleague from work act as DJ during your reception. Make sure he or she has experience with this sort of thing, and then set up your own sound system and your favorite CDs and let him or her go to work as a favor or gift to you. You can make your own music mixes for this volunteer DJ to play. Alternate fun songs with slow ones, traditional ethnic music with party classics, so that all your favorites are played at your reception.

~ If you're not a good music mixer, have a friend burn some songs onto DVDs and use those for the wedding.

~ Don't just turn on a CD player in the corner of the room. See if the reception hall has a way of hooking your music up to their sound system.

~ See if your reception hall is able to pipe into the room their own prerecorded dance music.

Dancing Lessons

~ You'll read in the bridal magazines, and friends will make the suggestion, to consider taking professional dancing lessons so that you'll look good on the dance floor. But professional dance lessons, even adult courses given at night at the high school, cost money. Instead, rent a video on ballroom dancing. Learn the basic steps you'll need to get through the spotlight dance and practice together for a while.

~ Enlist the aid of your light-footed parents or grandparents to help you both learn how to do a waltz or the cha-cha. Then, in turn, you can teach them how to do today's line dances. You'll have lots of fun learning together and showing off your new skills at the party.

32

Wedding Favors

Giving your guests a little something to remember your day is a lovely tradition and way to say thank you for sharing in the celebration. With all of the favor options out there, you'll find everything from over-the-top presents that raise eyebrows to embarrassingly cheap-looking items that hit the trash bin right away. Avoid making either mistake by choosing the right favors at the right prices.

Average Spending for Wedding Favors

2008	2009	2010	2011	2012	2013
$342	$352	$362	$372	$383	$394

Printed with permission from TheWeddingReport.com.

$\mathcal{E}$dible Favors

$\sim$ The usual sugar-coated almonds wrapped in tulle and ribbons can turn into a costly venture. Shop around for the almonds in different markets such as craft stores—not bridal specialty stores, gourmet food markets, or Italian bakeries where the prices are often triple.

$\sim$ Godiva chocolates *are* affordable at less than five dollars a box.

$\sim$ Go to a bulk candy store and purchase several pounds of colorful candies such as jelly beans, chocolate-covered nuts, and treats from your childhood as affordable options.

$\sim$ Cookies, brownies, and bars (lemon, streusel, blondies, etc.) are also excellent, popular favors. Just be sure to buy them from a grocery store or Costco and not from a pricey specialty cookie company online where prices are astronomical. They can also be made on the cheap.

$\sim$ Buy a few containers of microwave chocolate dipping sauce (the kind that hardens when you dip fruit into it, found in the produce section of most grocery stores for less than three dollars per canister), and make chocolate-dipped cookies such as Oreos.

～ Personalized M&Ms at mms.com, where you can choose your own color combinations and messages on the candies, do cost a bit per bag, but it turns out to be an economical choice when you divide the candies into little tulle pouches found at the craft store on the cheap.

Compare and Save
Candy pouches at bridal websites.................$2 each
Candy pouches at craft stores.......$4 for a pack of 10–12

～ Homemade chocolate candies packaged in little gift boxes are an economical choice, and you can attach to them the symbolism of the sweetness of marriage. It's not uncommon for brides to make these favors for less than twenty-five dollars for all the boxes they'll need.

～ The wine bottles with the personalized labels are out—which is a good thing because they are expensive.

Entertainment-Themed Favors

~ Visit kateaspen.com to stock up on favors used in entertaining, such as themed bottle openers and wine stoppers.

~ Coasters are great favors. Find these at home decor stores like Bed Bath & Beyond and at Target, Wal-Mart, Kohl's, and Marshalls, as well as at craft stores for pricing less than three dollars for sets of four.

Living Favors

~ Check nurseries and the flowers section of your grocery store for mini potted flowers at less than three dollars apiece.

~ Check your local garden center for potted kitchen herbs like basil, flat-leaf parsley, rosemary, and thyme at just a few dollars apiece, and wrap the pots in colorful foil papers found at the craft store.

~ For a "green" favor, give out packets of plant seeds from Home Depot for a dollar or two per pack.

Favors and Gifts Sources

Beverly Clark Collection—beverlyclark.com

Chandler's Candle Company—chandlerscandle.com

Double T Limited—uniquefavors.com

Exclusively Weddings—exclusivelyweddings.com

Forever and Always Company—foreverandalways.com

Gift Emporia.com—giftemporia.com

Godiva—godiva.com

Gratitude—giftsofgratitude.com

Kate Aspen—kateaspen.com

The Knot—theknot.com

Kohl's—kohls.com

M&Ms—mms.com

Personal Creations—personalcreations.com

Target—target.com

Tree and Floral Beginnings (seedlings, bulbs, and candles)—
   plantamemory.com; in Canada, plantamemory.on.ca

Wedding Solutions—weddingsolutions.com

Favors for the Home

∾ Many of today's brides are giving their guests small silver frames as favors. For a bulk discount, check your local craft store for pretty mini frames.

～ Framed poems are a great craft that allows you to personalize a message to your guests. Just add your self-printed poetry to those silver frames.

～ Scented candles are a great buy at craft stores, often at one-third the price found at home decor stores.

Additional Favor Ideas

～ Theme wedding favors easily can be made using supplies found at your local craft store. One bride with a beach-themed wedding (held, of course, at the beach) gifted her guests with a small glass bowl (ninety-nine cents each) filled with an inch or two of sand (four dollars for a large bag) and a few seashells and dried starfish (up to ninety-nine cents per piece). So each beach-theme favor cost less than five dollars, and they were beautiful.

～ If you'll donate to charity in lieu of favors, it's still a great idea to give guests a little something, such as a chocolate lollipop or a Hershey's Kiss attached to the donation card. At one wedding, the couple gave out one-dollar Lance Armstong Live Strong bracelets to their guests as part of their announcement that this was their chosen charity.

∾ Little poetry or quote gift books from the bookstore are great favors that you can purchase for less than five dollars each—ask the bookstore owner for a bulk discount if you're buying more than twenty, and you may see some big savings!

33

Keepsakes

It's great to have keepsakes of your big day, but you don't need to invest in some of the marketing gimmicks that are available today. You can create your own or your loved ones' keepsakes at a fraction of catalog costs, and they will have more personalized meaning.

⁓ To record your planning experiences—which are always fun to look back on—keep a journal in a plain, lined notebook. The fancy bridal journals on the market are not one page longer than these, and they do the same job, yet they may be double or triple in cost.

> **Compare and Save**
>
> Bridal journal ....$30–$40
>
> Plain journal.............................$5–$10

⌒ Charge up your personal home video camera and take your own footage throughout the wedding planning months and on the morning of the wedding. It's ridiculous to shell out the money for a professional photographer to record your rehearsal and the four hours it takes to get everyone ready before the ceremony. Besides, home movies are far more personal and fun than those taken by a stranger.

⌒ Make your own wedding memorabilia scrap box, where you can save swatches of material, favors, menus, invitations, and all the little meaningful items you wouldn't dare throw away. Bridal stores do sell these types of decorated memorabilia boxes, but you can beat their prices by covering a large cardboard box with either satiny material or bridal wrapping paper, lace, ribbons, bows, and a print label of the contents.

Compare and Save
Store-bought memorabilia box.................. $40–$60
Homemade box............................... $5–$20

〜 If you don't have room or enough keepsakes for a memorabilia box, make your own wedding scrapbook instead. Again, you'll do better to make your own rather than to buy one in a bridal store. You can keep all the notes, swatches, samples of perfume, and pictures you'll treasure years from now in this book.

Compare and Save
Store-bought bridal scrapbook.................. $20–$30
Homemade bridal scrapbook .... $10–$15

〜 Save copies of the letters you've written to update your bridal party and the letters you and your fiancé have written to one another during the planning of your wedding. No need for those specially ordered computer-printed love notes you can buy through catalogs. The real thing will do fine.

 ‿ If your photo store offers double prints for the same price as singles, or a free enlargement, take the opportunity to save money on prints you'd otherwise have to make for relatives and friends anyway.

 ‿ Printed napkins and matchboxes are nonessential keepsakes that can be cut out. If you desire these, however, take extra care to comparison shop in discount stationery stores and at print shops to get the best bargain possible. Include in your price research those items that may be offered by the reception hall as well. In some instances, they may even be offered as freebies. Check well.

34

Wedding Night Accommodations

You'll certainly want to spend your first night together in memorable surroundings. Use this chapter to plan your wedding night accommodations for less.

∼ Get a plain old regular room, instead of the honeymoon suite or presidential suite. Do you really need to pay three times as much for designer furniture, nice artwork, a scenic view, and a hot tub in the bathroom? You'll probably be exhausted after the excitement of the day, and all the facilities and extras may be lost on you. Besides, it's the first night of your honeymoon. You won't be looking at the view or admiring the artwork anyway.

∼ If you'll have to catch a flight at a faraway airport early the next morning, you may choose to spend the night at a hotel near there. Airport-access hotels are often overpriced due to demand, so you'll definitely want to get a no-frills room there. The honeymoon suite will be too costly.

~ See if you can get your first night's room for free as part of the group discount in the hotel in which your visiting family and friends are staying. One bride negotiated a free night's stay in the hotel, saving $250.

~ If you have your own place, why not spend the first night there? After all, it's free, and your first night together can make those familiar surroundings new and exciting.

~ Perhaps friends or relatives can let you use their guest cottage. It can be their wedding gift to you.

~ However, if you just won't have it any other way—if you must have the honeymoon suite—comparison shop around town. You can at least find the lowest price available.

~ The first night spent in a luxury hotel is a great gift idea for parents to consider. They may have wanted to pay for your honeymoon, but they'll be happy you've found them this equally special gesture at less of a blow to their savings. Discuss this idea with them, or with any other relative or friend who might find this an appropriate gift—perhaps the people who introduced you.

35

Your Trousseau

While you're having fun on your honeymoon you might as well look your best. You could max out your credit cards to buy new vacation outfits and accessories, but this is not a fashion show. Many brides have shared their trousseau secrets with me; after seeing their honeymoon photos I couldn't agree more that they made the economically correct clothing decisions. This chapter will help you decide on the right purchases for your trip, so you can have something new without an expense that you'll be paying off forever.

~ You don't have to buy a whole new wardrobe. That may have been the case in the old days, but now it's smarter to just buy a few special new pieces and fill in the gaps with your favorite vacation clothes and shoes.

~ Buy clothing you can use again. Onetime wearings aren't worth the ticket price.

～ Stay away from top-name, high-priced clothing stores. Why get one item for two hundred dollars when you can get five great new things for the same price elsewhere?

～ Don't shop in bridal boutiques for your honeymoon outfits and lingerie. Go to regular department stores and mid-priced lingerie boutiques instead for better choices and better prices.

～ Throughout the year, and especially during the winter holiday season when summer clothes are still available on clothing websites' clearance sections, take advantage of big sales that can save you 40 to 60 percent on bathing suits, cover-ups, shoes, dresses, and fitness clothing for active adventures during your honeymoon.

～ Don't overbuy, using your honeymoon as an excuse to splurge on yourself. Of course, the temptation will be there, but act in moderation. Consider the money you save to be money in your airfare fund.

～ If you have shoes that are in good condition and are suitable for your vacation, use them. Besides the money you save, you're also saving the pain and trouble of breaking in new shoes during your getaway. There's no time for blisters on a honeymoon.

～ Shop at discount stores and in outlets for incredible bargains in your area.

∽ Don't shop for your trousseau until after your bridal showers. You just may get all the lingerie and robes you'll ever need as gifts. One bride originally budgeted two hundred dollars for her honeymoon lingerie. After receiving a roomful of teddies and bustiers, she redirected that money to her attendants' gifts.

∽ Pamper yourself with new lingerie and undergarments more than with outer clothing. A trousseau fund spent mostly on teddies and garters will make for a more interesting trip than new shorts and earrings.

Your Going-Away Outfit

∽ Instead of buying a brand-new, expensive dress specifically for the trip from the reception to the airport (or from the reception to the hotel), use one of your honeymoon dresses.

∽ Perhaps your going-away dress can be a gift from your mother or grandmother.

∽ Or just make your grand exit from the reception in your wedding gown, and then change at home into casual clothes for more comfortable traveling to the airport or hotel. You won't even need a going-away outfit.

36

Guest Lodging

If you have guests coming in from out of town, you might choose to pay for their lodging expenses. Learn how to find suitable accommodations for them with your budget in mind, plus treat them a little with the savings you've found.

⌁ Comparison shop for the best-priced hotels in town, taking care not to book a dive just because of its low prices. A room in a cockroach-infested truck stop is no way to welcome your favorite people. So look around, ask to see the rooms, and talk to people who are actually staying at the hotel.

⌁ A good idea is to book the rooms in the hotel where the reception is being held. That way, no one has to get in a car and drive after the party. You can often get discount prices for rooms booked in that hotel.

〜 Ask about group rates for hotel room blocks. It doesn't cost you anything to set up a room block for your estimated number of guests, and you may earn 10 to 20 percent off the hotel's regular rates for your guests. It's up to them to book their own reservations, so share the discount information on your wedding website. Book room blocks at a range of hotels around town, in low to moderate price ranges, so that guests can book whatever fits their budget.

〜 Don't let these guests come into town too early. Two days ahead of time is more than enough. You don't want to have to entertain them while there's so much for you to do, and unnecessary days' accommodations just rack up extra hotel bills. Make it clear that everyone is to arrive only a day or two before the wedding.

〜 If there aren't too many people coming in from out of town, they might choose to stay with relatives or friends rather than booking hotel rooms. You can't ask for volunteers—but don't volunteer your place. That's just too much craziness underfoot when you have so much to do.

 ∼ Suggest that guests stay in bed-and-breakfasts near the wedding location. These are often priced lower than brand-name hotels, and breakfast is included. Visit bnbfinder.com to locate great B&Bs.

 ∼ Contact your own local tourism department (yes, you can do that!). They often have coupon packets, passes for free admission to museums, free train or bus passes, freebies for the kids, and information packets that you can get for your guests. Visit towd.com to find your wedding location's local tourism bureau.

 ∼ Place inexpensive gifts in your guests' rooms. Good ideas are baskets of soft drinks and snacks, maps and listings of interesting things to see and do in the area, and toys and games for the kids. Always include a personal note, thanking your guests for coming to town.

37

The Rehearsal Dinner

Here's where it all starts to come together. The plans are set and it's walk-through time. After the rehearsal, once everyone gets their places and lines in order, you'll head off for your last party as engaged people. The rehearsal dinner is a festive event with everyone sharing in the excitement, proposing toasts, and looking forward to the next day. You can help plan a memorable dinner on any budget. Here are some ideas for you to consider.

~ Your informal rehearsal dinner could be a pizza party, a barbecue in the yard, a pool party, a picnic, or any other inexpensive style of gathering. Obviously, ordering six pizzas is going to cost a lot less than throwing a clambake for fifteen people, so look toward budget-priced menus.

∿ You can still have a sit-down dinner. Just serve it at home instead of at a fancy restaurant. Choose from inexpensive meals that stretch to feed a crowd: pasta, stew, Mexican fare, home-made pizzas set up in a make-your-own arrangement.

∿ Plan the menu carefully. At a restaurant, offer a choice of two or three preselected, reasonably priced menu items rather than allowing guests to order whatever they'd like off the menu. That keeps lobster off the tab, and your prix fixe menu allows you to choose a dollar limit per guest, as allowed by a pasta dish and a chicken dish for the meal.

∿ Skip the appetizers for a group at a restaurant. Just serve salad and an entrée. That can cut hundreds off your dining bill.

∿ Skip dessert at the restaurant, which might run you ten dollars per person. Instead, take your group to an ice cream parlor for three-dollar cones and shakes, coffee floats, and other fun treats. Or plan to offer an inexpensive dessert for your rehearsal dinner guests. A tray of brownies is a winning option, as are homemade cupcakes, a platter of cookies (even store-bought), or a homemade or Entenmann's apple pie with ice cream. These "tastes of childhood" are not only inexpensive beyond belief, they add a personalized touch to the celebration.

~ Shop at Costco for inexpensive party platters, frozen hors d'oeuvres, and desserts.

~ Close relatives who volunteer may bring their famous prepared entrée or dessert as a contribution to the meal. If it's a favorite recipe, ask the cook to provide you with a recipe for sharing with the guests.

~ Preselect wine and beverage items as well, rather than allowing guests to order pricey drinks and shots. If you're holding an informal rehearsal dinner, pitchers of beer and soda are fine in addition to moderately priced bottles of wine.

~ Have dessert and coffee at a nice café. The term *rehearsal dinner* doesn't have to mean dinner. Guests love it when you plan a unique celebration like this, and they get a range of tasty treats.

~ Skip the professional photographer. While you'll undoubtedly want some record of this gathering, it's enough to take your own shots or get copies of those taken by your family and friends. There's no need to spend five hundred dollars for a professional photo session of the rehearsal dinner.

38

Your Personal Beauty Care

The bride deserves the royal treatment on her wedding day. It's possible to get all the pampering and primping you need while still respecting your budget. Learn how to create a gorgeous wedding day look at little cost.

～ Don't buy all new makeup just for your wedding. You're better off using your customary makeup for the more natural look you're used to. Some less frugal brides have reported dropping $125 on glamour-line cosmetics. The rest of us could find a better use for that money.

～ Scout out the makeup counters for free samples for you and your bridesmaids. Just one of those little tubes of lipstick is enough to keep you in the pink throughout your wedding day. Just don't attempt to grab fourteen of those little samples.

There's a difference between making good use of a sample and taking advantage.

∼ Do your own makeup. After all, you'll do the most natural-looking job on yourself. A professional might overpaint you . . . and then expect to be paid for the stuff you'll just wipe off later anyway. Besides, some brides find it relaxing to do their own makeup on their wedding day. Just give yourself plenty of time.

Compare and Save
Professional makeup application . . . . $90–$120
Do it yourself. . . . . free

∼ If you've always dyed your hair and you're comfortable with the way it turns out every time, then there's no reason you shouldn't do your own touch-ups rather than go to a salon.

Compare and Save
Salon dye job. . . . . $80–$200
At-home dye job . . . . $10–$15

∿ Few brides would take the chance of cutting their own hair just for the money saved. A good haircut is the basis of the bride's style, and it's also an inexpensive way to get that pampered feeling without the full line of extravagances. So the best way to watch your finances when it comes to haircuts is simply to stay with your regular stylist. A too-cheap salon you've found on a back road may give terrible, disastrous haircuts, and a gaudy, overpriced one may give you a standard chop with an outrageous bill attached. The best way to save money on your haircut: just have a wash and cut instead of the wash, cut, and style.

∿ Have a bridesmaid or even a neighbor French braid your hair for you if you like the look but can't do it yourself. The favor saves you salon prices, which can run up to ninety dollars for this simple service!

∿ Have a bridesmaid pin your headpiece on for you. Why would you need to go to a salon for that and then have to drive home with your headpiece on?

∿ Use your own home waxing kit rather than go to a salon for hair removal, if you have experience waxing yourself. Never try an at-home job for the first time right before your wedding, or you could experience skin irritation or injury. If you're experienced and choose to self-wax, savings can reach anywhere from thirty to more than one hundred dollars.

⌒ Do your own nails. And if you like the look of a French manicure, practice on yourself using a French manicure kit. The big new trend is simple pink fingernails and toenails, requiring no steady hand with the French manicure white polish.

Compare and Save
Salon nails. . . . . $20–$50
Home job. . . . . free

⌒ Advise your maids to do their makeup, waxing, tanning, and manicures for themselves as well. They'll save money, and you won't wind up with any cosmetic nightmares walking down the aisle ahead of you.

As cost effective as these tips are, you may still find it worth the expense to go for the royal treatment at your beauty salon. In fact, many brides and their bridal parties say the morning spent at the salon enjoying the full bridal package did much to ease their nerves and make them feel more beautiful than if they had done the jobs themselves. They wouldn't trade the experience. Of course there's nothing wrong with that. Your salon may offer you their wedding morning package at a price that's right for you.

∼ You can enjoy the salon treatment for less than the bridal package deal, though. Do you all need facials? It may not be a good idea to have one right before the wedding, in case of irritation. Do you all need pedicures? Massages? Color analysis? Espresso and continental breakfast? Make a deal with the salon owner instead for you to get a group rate for hair stylings and—if you choose—manicures. The package deal you work out for yourself will undoubtedly be much less expensive. One bride negotiated her bridal beauty package down fifty dollars per person. You could do the same.

∼ Ask your beauty salon manager if you can bring in your own breakfast and champagne for your bridal party members. Some establishments will grant permission for your own personal buffet in a private room.

Beauty Emergency Kit
Prepare an emergency kit with clear nail polish, a small sewing kit, pain reliever, a nail file, club soda, extra lipstick and face powder, and even a stapler for last-minute mishaps and touchups. Have someone keep it in his or her car or take it to the reception.

39

Gifts for Others

Your loved ones have given you a gift by attending your wedding, help-ing you plan it, or helping pay for it. Show them how much you appre-ciate those actions with a gift they'll cherish forever. You can spend a fortune on your selections, but the meaning counts more than the price. Read on for some ideas on how to choose the perfect gift for everyone on your list.

〜 Don't buy the fancy thank-you gifts sold in bridal salons and bridal catalogs. By now you know you can do much bet-ter than that. Instead, look for sales in local stores, online, and in gift catalogs for items your loved ones will really be able to use. Holiday and end-of-season sales often turn up phenome-nal price cuts.

Average Spending for Gifts

	2008	2009	2010	2011	2012	2013
For attendants	$429	$441	$453	$465	$478	$491
For each other	$470	$483	$496	$510	$524	$538
For parents	$186	$191	$196	$201	$207	$213
From guests	$96	$99	$102	$105	$108	$111

Ninety-nine percent of couples polled research gifts online, and 39 percent purchase online.

Printed with permission from TheWeddingReport.com.

~ Look in your local discount store such as Target or Wal-Mart for low-priced music CDs, coffee-table books, spa socks and robe sets, and other choices.

~ Take advantage of sales at Victoria's Secret and other women's loungewear catalogs and get plush robes for nineteen dollars, comfy socks for six dollars per set, nightshirts in bright colors for twelve dollars, and perfume or lotion sets for less than twenty dollars as an indulgent gift for your bridesmaids.

Popular Gift Ideas

Some of the top gift items are travel related such as luggage tags or passport cases (less than fifteen dollars), home related such as marble coaster sets (less than twenty dollars) and espresso cup sets (less than ten dollars), photo related such as pretty silver frames from the craft store (eight dollars during a 40-percent-off sale!), candles and pretty glass holders or ceramic bases (less than twenty dollars), scent diffuser vases with reeds (less than fifteen dollars), spa robes (less than fifty dollars), and stylish tote bags for vacationing (less than twenty-five dollars).

⁓ Groomsmen don't need that pricey silver flask engraved with their names. They want something they can use or look at all the time, so check craft stores for unique architectural photo frames and fill them with great "guy photos" from the wedding day. If your proof prints are free, you've just spent five dollars on a frame.

⁓ A no-fail gift: a nice bottle of wine. Visit winespectator .com for a list of wines for less than thirty dollars, perfect for budget-priced gift giving.

∼ Look also at well-priced flavored rums and other unique liquors, plus liqueurs and after-dinner drinks as a gift that the recipient will use and enjoy in the future.

∼ Photo albums are terrific wedding gifts, especially when filled with a selection of those free proof prints or ten-cent Kodak prints off your digital camera. Visit Target, Kohl's, Wal-Mart, and other budget stores for a selection of pretty styles.

∼ Consider gift certificates for makeovers, golf games, lingerie, CDs, even home repair and babysitting services. These, of course, will not be kept forever, but they'll certainly be appreciated as thoughtful gifts. Plus they can be found at low prices—some for no price if you're doing the offering on that babysitting gig.

∼ For kids' gifts, get them a low-denomination (twenty dollars) gift card to their favorite store, such as Target or a toy store, so that they can pick out the game they want, music they like, a stuffed animal, a book, or tween hair accessories. It's the shopping trip that's the real treat.

∼ Have baskets filled with midnight munchies delivered to your family's and friends' hotel rooms after the reception. You can make all the cookies, brownies, and candies yourself and have a friend make the delivery after you've left for your honeymoon. Members of more rowdy bridal parties who are planning to continue the celebration long into the night will appreciate your sending over several bottles of champagne . . . or the leftovers from the reception!

~ Not to be dismissed is the handwritten thank-you note. A personal letter is always treasured and is priceless.

Author's Note

Of course, there are many more ways to save money on your wedding than the ideas mentioned here. You may have near you a fabulous source of materials or flowers, a great craft store, a metropolitan area with a diamond district or a row of whole-salers, and you may live in a region that offers more moderate prices for wedding services than other areas do. You might have talented volunteers who can make anything from your table linens to your wedding cake. Your own personal advantages are endless, once you start looking around and thinking outside the usual way of doing things.

With this book, you've learned to spend your money with quality in mind, with a deeper understanding of the unique ways the wedding industry works, and you've also learned how to protect your investments and to keep organized. That gives you a big advantage over uninformed brides and grooms, when you're making the right choices and asking the right questions. It's my hope that these tips allow you to bring your full wedding dream to life, that you don't have to sacrifice any part of your wedding wishes, and that your entire family and bridal party will join you in cutting down wedding expenses. A wedding is supposed to be fun, so when you're all sharing your big budget victories and finding yourselves able to say yes to the things you want, you're bringing the joy back into the process and not letting the money get you down.

You've become a smarter, savvier wedding shopper, and I'm confident that you'll save plenty of money on your pre-wedding activities, ceremony, reception, and honeymoon—all without the savings showing to any of your guests. And that once-dreaded wedding budget will turn into something you're very proud of.

You'll also be proud to save a fortune on your honeymoon! For a free bonus chapter to this book, visit sharonnaylor.net and get ninety-two tips on planning and enjoying the perfect post-wedding getaway!

Best of luck on your wedding and in your new life together!

—Sharon Naylor

Index

Accessories, 50, 130–38, 147, 148, 151, 157
Aisle runner, 214
Albums, 243–45, 350
Alterations, 123, 125, 144
Announcements, 2–5
At-home cards, 191

Bands, 10, 36, 79, 306–13
Beauty care, 40, 341–45
Best man, 31–32, 42, 48
Better Business Bureau, 26–27, 118, 171, 239, 272
Beverages, 8, 70, 270, 285–90, 339. *See also* Liquor
Bouquets, 209–12
Bridal party, 47–51
    communicating with, 30–32
    dressing, 139–51
    transportation for, 229–31

Bridal salons, 3, 110–11, 113, 116, 148, 154–55, 156, 191, 261, 292, 302, 347
Bridal shows, 33–37
Bridesmaids, 29, 31–32, 118, 128–29, 139–48, 212
Budget, 53–60

Cake, 291–98, 300–303
Cake cutter, 302–3
Cake-top decorations, 300–302
Calligraphy, 188–89, 256
Candles, 217, 218, 263, 264
Car rentals, 223, 227–28
Cash bar, 285
Catering, 7, 66, 107, 269–72, 280–81, 292. *See also* Food
    average prices, 59
    self-, 282–83
Centerpieces, 217–22

Ceremony, 233–35
  elements in, 101–8
  flowers for, 214–15
  location of, 83–91, 96
Charitable donations, 44, 320
Children, 76–77, 350
Chocolate fountain, 299
Chocolate sculpture, 267
Christmas lights, 220–21, 266
Chuppah, 214
Coffee, 290, 298
Computers, do-it-yourself projects on,
  4–5, 21–22, 56, 186–87, 189,
  256–57
Contracts, 23–25, 98, 163, 226, 245,
  253, 311
Corkage fees, 288
Corsages, 212
Cultural elements, 107–8

Dancing lessons, 314
Day of the week for wedding, 67–68
Dead stock, 287
Deadlines, recording, 28
Decorations, 10–11, 215–16, 265–68
Delivery charges, 99, 213, 293
Desserts, 9, 298–300
Destination weddings, 75, 195–99
Discontinued gown styles, 112, 141
Discounts, 58, 95–96
  bridesmaids' dresses, 142
  cake, 292
  destination wedding, 197
  employee, 117, 170
  flowers, 203–4
  limousine, 227
  lodging, 328, 334
  photos, 249
  rings, 169
  shoes, 128, 146, 157, 164
  tuxedos, 160, 161, 165
Divorce or annulment, proof of, 105

DJ, 10, 36, 79, 306, 307–12, 313
Duty-free shopping, 170

E-mail, 31, 32, 192, 194
Engagement, 1–11
  announcements, 2–5
  party, 6–11

Fathers, 159–64
Favors, 11, 219, 315–21
Flower girls, 48, 148–51, 262
Flowers, 65–66, 86, 198, 201–17, 218
  average spending on, 203
  cost-free possibilities, 201–2
  shopping tips, 206–13
  sources of, 203–5
Food, 59, 66, 75, 107, 269–83. *See also*
  Cake; Catering
  average cost of, 69
  for children, 76–77
  for engagement party, 7–8
  for rehearsal dinner, 337–39
  for service providers, 79
  suggested choices, 272–81
Formality of wedding, 59, 68–69, 120,
  121, 154, 179, 269–70
Freebies, 35, 37, 54, 58, 86, 197, 234,
  267, 341–42

Garter, 130, 136
Gift cards, 39–40, 41, 136, 197–98, 350
Gift lists, 39–40
Gifts for others, 347–51
Gloves, 137, 148
Gowns and dresses
  brides', 109–25, 198
  bridesmaids', 29, 50, 118, 139–45
  flower girls', 148–50
  mothers', 140, 153–56
Groom, 36, 40, 135, 159–64
Groom's cake, 297
Groomsmen, 159–64, 349

Guest book, 261–63
Guest list, 30, 59, 73–81
  "and guests," 77–79
  cutting down, 79–81
  organizing, 74–75

Hairstyling, 40, 110, 198, 342–43, 345
Handfasting, 106
Headpieces, 133–35, 150, 157, 343
Home weddings, 89–90
Honeymoon, 64, 197. *See also*
  Destination weddings
Honeymoon registries, 43, 197–98
Horse and carriage rides, 228

Ice sculpture, 267
Insurance, 45, 95, 177, 199
Invitations, 44, 179–90, 194
  average spending on, 180
  choosing the right style, 182–84
  engagement party, 6
  resources for, 181

Jewelry, 137–38, 148, 151, 157. *See also*
  Rings
Journal, wedding, 323–24

Keepsakes, 323–26

Limousines, 37, 223, 224–27, 229–30
Lingerie, 40, 135–37, 330, 331
Liquor, 8, 270, 285–89, 290, 339, 350
List making, 27, 28
Location
  ceremony, 83–91, 96
  reception, 93–99
Lodging/accommodations
  for the bride and groom, 327–28
  for guests, 50, 65, 81, 333–35

Maid/matron of honor, 31–32, 42, 48
Mailing lists, 35

Makeup, 110, 341–42
Manicures, 344, 345
Maps and directions, 192–93
Measurements and sizes, 31–32, 123,
  125, 144, 161
Memorabilia box, 324–25
Men, dressing, 159–65
Menu cards, 259
Money gifts, 43, 45, 55
Mortgage registries, 43
Mothers, 140, 153–57, 212–13
Music, 305–14. *See also* Bands; DJ
  average spending on, 306
  for the ceremony, 84, 104–5, 106,
    107, 233–35
  for the engagement party, 10
  mix-and-match format, 308

Name change, 191
Newspaper announcements, 2–3

Officiant, 84–85, 101–3, 105, 201–2,
  233
Organization, 19–23
Outdoor weddings, 86–88, 96, 235
Outlet stores, 119, 128, 143, 146, 149,
  156, 162, 164, 330

Parents, 13, 14–15, 42, 55–56, 73–74,
  80. *See also* Fathers; Mothers
Parking, 94
Party bus, 37, 230
Permits, 87
Photography, 94–95, 104, 237–49, 326.
  See also Videography
  average cost of, 237, 238
  at the ceremony, 84
  engagement, 1, 9–10
  one-time-use cameras, 9–10, 247–48
  rehearsal dinner, 339
Place cards, 255, 258
Premarital classes, 105

Professional associations, 26
Programs, 191, 255–58
Prom dresses/season, 128, 133, 143, 155, 161

Receipts, keeping, 21, 25, 124, 163, 186, 245, 281, 312
Reception location, 93–99
Registries, 40–45, 197–98
Rehearsal dinner, 337–39
Religious elements, 84–85, 103–5
Rentals
    car, 223, 227–28
    for ceremony, 85, 87
    extra fees, 71, 98
    for home weddings, 90
    limousine, 223, 224–27, 229–30
    for reception, 93–94, 97–99
    shoes, 164
    tuxedo, 160–61, 165
    wedding gown, 119
Response cards, 184
Ring bearers, 165, 262
Ring pillows, 263
Rings, 167–77
    average spending on, 168
    company websites, 172
    design choices, 173–77
    investment protection tips, 177
RSVPs, 30
Rush fees, avoiding, 19, 29, 32, 161

Sample sales, 111, 112
Samples, 29, 35, 341–42
Sashes, 148
Save-the-date cards, 193–94
Schedule, wedding, 31
Scrapbooks, 325
Season and date of wedding, 61–66. See also Weather

Shoes, 127–30, 145–47, 150, 156–57, 164, 165, 330
Shuttle service, 230–31, 232
Site fees, 94
Spiritual elements, 105–6
Sponsored weddings, 60
Stationery, 3–5, 180, 191
Stockings, 136–37
Suits, 160–64, 165

Teenagers, 77
Telephone number list, 28
Thank-you notes, 191–92, 351
Theme weddings, 267, 320
Time of wedding, 68–71
Transportation, 223–32
Travel, 50, 64–65, 70, 81, 102. See also Lodging/accommodations
Trousseau, 329–31
Trunk sales, 111, 114, 131, 137, 141, 148
Tuxedos, 50, 160–63, 164, 165

Unity candles, 263, 264
Ushers, 31–32, 48

Veil, 130–33
Vendors, communicating with, 23–27
Videography, 104, 237, 238, 250–54, 324

Waxing, body, 343
Weather, 64, 70, 87, 96. See also Season and date of wedding
Wedding consultants, 58
Wedding coordinators, 15, 79, 86
Wedding planning books/organizers, 19–23
Wedding websites, 18–19, 22, 193, 194